Home Decor

A *Sunset* Design Guide

w/D

by Kerrie L. Kelly and the Editors of Sunset Books

Contents

Decorating your home is about more than just filling the rooms with furniture and accessories. Your home's decor should reflect your style and taste, with personal touches that help set it apart. It should be welcoming to you, your family, and your guests. Most of all, it should be a place you're proud of.

Achieving this goal can be tricky. Discovering what style appeals to you, choosing colors, finding the right furniture, and adding accessories and finishing touches take time and can seem overwhelming. Added to this is the need to plan a schedule and budget.

We're here to help. On these pages, we've amassed photos, information, and expert advice to help you design all the rooms inside your house...and outside as well. The result will be a home that makes the most of your space and enhances your quality of life.

ISBN-13: 978-0-376-01352-1
ISBN-10: 0-376-01352-4
Library of Congress Control
Number: 2008942471

10 9 8 7 6 5 4 3 2 1
First Printing July 2009
Printed in the United States of America

OXMOOR HOUSE, INC.
VP, Publishing Director: Jim Childs
Brand Manager: Fonda Hitchcock
Managing Editor: L. Amanda Owens
Project Editor: Diane Rose

Home Decor: A Sunset Design Guide
CONTRIBUTORS
Author: Kerrie L. Kelly
Developmental Editor: Marianne Lipanovich
Consulting Editors: Bob Doyle,
Carrie Dodson Davis
Production Specialist: Linda M. Bouchard
Prepress Coordinator: Eligio Hernández
Copy Editor: Carol Whiteley
Proofreader: Denise Griffiths
Intern: Emily Chappell
Indexer: Marjorie Joy
Series Designer: Vasken Guiragossian

To order additional publications,
call 1-800-765-6400

For more books to enrich your life,
visit oxmoorhouse.com

Visit Sunset online at sunset.com

For the most comprehensive selection of
Sunset books, visit sunsetbooks.com

For more exciting home and garden ideas,
visit myhomeideas.com

Cover Photo: Photography by Eric Roth;
design by Two Ton, Inc.

Design Panel

The following design and building professionals from across the United States lent their enormous talent and valuable advice to the pages of this book.

Michael Hennessey
FURNITURE DESIGNER

Michael Hennessey became enamored with furniture after finding himself in a factory in Indonesia. He was struck by the honesty and skill that could be put into the simplest of pieces. His company, C.G. Sparks, has been the perfect avenue for bringing antiques and new designs from around the world to the United States since 2002. At C.G. Sparks, everyone wholeheartedly believes that each piece's spirit is shared with its surroundings. History, craftsmanship, and materials all lend themselves to creating a piece that is greater than the sum of its parts.
cgsparks.com

Jennifer Hilgardner
INTERIOR DESIGNER

Jennifer Hilgardner lives on the West Coast, but never lost her Southeastern roots. She has a BS in Business and a degree in Interior Design, which gave her the background to launch her own design firm, Timeless Design and Accents. Her work reflects her ability to blend design styles to come up with the end result the client envisions.
timelessdesignandaccents.com

Virginia Young and Janie Lowe ("YO + LO")
PAINT SPECIALISTS

Self-described "color nerds," Virginia Young and Janie Lowe made a commitment to use paint and plaster products that have a lower impact on their own health, their clients' health, and the environment. They started in the paint world as owners of a custom paint and plaster finishes company in 1996, and in 2005 launched YOLO Colorhouse, providing environmentally responsible paint with a natural palette. Minneapolis native Virginia, who holds a degree in Fine Arts from Colorado College, continued her education in graphic design at the Portfolio Center in Atlanta. Janie received her degree in Fine Arts from Texas Tech University and then continued her education, receiving her Master of Fine Arts from the School of Visual Arts in New York City. | **yolocolorhouse.com**

Matt Lemos
LANDSCAPE DESIGNER

Matt Lemos is the principal of Lemos Landscape Company, a full-service Northern California landscape design/build firm. He has been involved in the landscape industry for over 15 years, including working as lead designer for a residential landscaping program with Del Webb Corporation, as a field supervisor, and as director of Warranty Operations. A native of the Sacramento Valley, Matt has unique concepts about outdoor living areas and space planning, which have been featured in numerous publications.

Tracy Bowman
TILE SPECIALIST

Tracy Bowman has 24 years of experience in the tile and stone industry. She has designed and remodeled showrooms and design studios, with an emphasis on eco-friendliness. Her passion is creating an environment that reflects the client's personality while maintaining a sense of style. | **nsdgallery.com**

Heather Loehr
TILE AND FLOORING SPECIALIST

Heather Loehr was born and raised in the tile and stone industry. Not only does she possess in-depth knowledge of a wide range of tile products, she also has a strong sense of design and great understanding of appropriate installation practices. Heather has helped to orchestrate the installation of millions of square feet of tile and stone for custom homes and commercial spaces across the West. | **nsdgallery.com**

Kyle Bunting
CREATIVE HIDE SPECIALIST

For almost a decade, Kyle Bunting has been redefining how hide is used in interior design. Through innovative hide rugs and wall coverings to an extensive upholstery collection, Kyle encourages and creates the extraordinary in hide. Since its inception, his company has completed thousands of projects throughout the world. Kyle has been published in countless periodicals, and was a 2007 Interior Design Product of the Year finalist. Today Kyle and his team of contributing designers find inspiration in his studio outside of Austin in Texas Hill Country. | **kylebunting.com**

Zack Rosson
LIGHTING SPECIALIST

Zack Rosson has been with Lumens Light + Living since 2006. He was educated in design in northern California, and his residential and hospitality work is now found throughout the Sacramento Valley. Zack believes that lighting is one of the most important aspects of interior design and that it is commonly overlooked. He feels that lighting should fulfill the utilitarian objectives of everyday life while complementing every decorative style—giving new meaning to the saying "Let there be light!" | **lumens.com**

Clay Aurell
ARCHITECT

Clay Aurell, AIA, earned a Bachelor of Architecture degree at California State Polytechnic University, Pomona, in 1997. He moved to Santa Barbara in 1998, where he began working with two top award-winning architectural design firms. In 2003, Clay began his own design practice, AB Design Studio, which has won local and national awards. He has also worked with the City of Santa Barbara and fellow community leaders to make a difference in the planning and policy efforts of the region. He and his firm participate in the 1% Program of Public Architecture as a way to give back to the community. | **aurellblumer.com**

John Slaughter
GENERAL CONTRACTOR

John Slaughter has been in the home construction industry for 20 years, working on thousands of homes throughout California. He earned a Bachelor of Science degree in Building Construction from Texas A&M University and has worked with numerous architects and interior designers throughout Nevada and California. His honors include earning the coveted National Housing Quality award from the National Association of Home Builders as a team leader. His company, Retroactive Home Construction, Inc., was created to focus on architecture from the 1940s, '50s, and '60s, updating that period's construction to exceed modern energy efficiency and building codes while preserving the architectural and design integrity of the home.

Chapter 1

Getting Started

What kind of place do you want to come home to? It should be a space that is comfortable, welcoming, and a reflection of your style and taste—one that is uniquely yours. The key to such a space is great design. Some people have a clear vision and are confident about decorating, while others find the prospect daunting. Whether you consider the process exciting or intimidating, the steps are the same—dream first, explore your options, then create a plan that will allow you to reach your goal, with enough flexibility in both plan and budget to allow for the unexpected.

Design Basics

There is no one way to design a room, nor one style that is best for any space. Good design is personal. Good rooms are livable, conveying the sense that the person who designed them made thoughtful aesthetic judgments about the elements within the space, and then embraced those judgments completely. Good rooms are harmonious. At the same time, they aren't predictable and don't slavishly follow one particular look.

The best rooms defy classification—and so do the best designers. Great rooms evolve as we live in them, reflecting the stories of our lives. But before you can design such rooms, you need to understand both the definitions of different interior styles and the main principles of design.

This means gaining basic knowledge of the elements present in different design styles. It also means understanding how to pull those elements together to create a space that is both functional and beautiful. These concepts apply whether you're decorating or redecorating an entire house or merely want to refresh a room with new wall color or upholstery. They can be used in any room in the house, from a large, formal living room to a humble mudroom. By understanding these definitions and principles, you'll understand why certain

spaces naturally appeal to you. Applying these principles in every space you design will help you create rooms that are exciting to look at, pleasing to be in, and welcoming to family and friends.

ABOVE Furniture lines, textures, flooring, and color choices all play a role in creating a well-designed room.

TOP RIGHT Even monochromatic spaces can support a little whimsy, such as this graphic carpet.

BOTTOM RIGHT Incorporating elements that are functional yet unexpected, such as this ladder to the loft, adds personality to even understated spaces.

An interesting thing happens when you ask people to describe their decorating styles. Often they freeze for a moment, caught in some sort of linguistic headlight, and then blurt out, "Um, I don't know—eclectic?"

Even designers do this. "Eclectic" has come to mean "I have my own personal style; I mix things together, old and new, classic and modern, things that I like." By being "eclectic," we resist being limited. We may make mistakes, but we keep trying until we settle into rooms that we feel express ourselves. Fortunately, today's best designs, even those with a specific "style," reflect this.

According to interior designer Jennifer Hilgardner, "A house becomes a home with the blend of styles. It brings the personalities of the family living there into the space." Just as it's humdrum to see someone dressed head to toe in one designer's clothing, it's uninspiring to see rooms that are based solely on one style. As soon as rooms start filling up with too many signature pieces from any one style, they become predictable and lose their appeal. Your eye scans those rooms and floats on, never focusing on any single point.

Sticking to a single set of rules may be out the window, but that doesn't necessarily mean anything goes—that is, not if you want rooms that are pleasing to others' eyes as well. Understanding the basic components of the three major "master" styles will help you lay the underpinnings for a well-designed room that reflects your personality and taste.

Although there are a seemingly unlimited number of highly specific design styles, a case can be made that these are the master styles: traditional, modern, and transitional. Understanding the basics of each of these styles will help you make appropriate decisions when designing your own rooms.

INTERIOR DESIGNER
JENNIFER HILGARDNER ON

Eclectic Style

I have seen more residential clients having an eclectic style. Some of the reasons are the blending of two families, bringing items home from travel, and purchasing a piece of art or furniture because they love it. This is what creates the mix-match style that shows personality and makes a house a home."

OPPOSITE PAGE Adding simple traditional trim pieces, including crown molding, baseboards, wainscoting, door casing, and ceiling details, makes a room feel richer. Here the contrasting paint draws additional attention to the detailing.

TOP You can easily pull off eclectic styling by keeping the color scheme in the same tone and the structural elements, such as these ceiling beams, consistent throughout, which helps tie everything together.

BOTTOM Using a harmonious flooring material throughout allows traditional pieces and modern elements to complement each other rather than clash. The sleek architectural lines of this contemporary kitchen are a backdrop that sets off heirloom furnishings.

TOP LEFT The classic architectural elements and full fabric window coverings seen here are hallmarks of traditional style. The updated fabric choices and warm-toned upholstery and wall colors give the style a fresh look.

BOTTOM LEFT Contrasting wall color and painted woodwork give this traditional dining room a welcome graciousness.

RIGHT Ironwork above the windows provides unique artwork while traditional fabrics bring richness. The dark hardwood flooring and wall sconces complement this stylized family room.

Traditional Elements

Without a doubt, traditional style remains at the top of America's popularity chart for home decorating. Gracious and inviting, traditional design evokes images of understated elegance. It offers the warmth and classical comfort many of us remember from our childhood homes. Within the "traditional" designation, you'll find specific styles, such as classic, colonial, Tuscan, and country.

If you equate "traditional" and "grand" with "old and stodgy," it's time to take another look at this style. Although traditional

design still reflects fine woodworking, craftsmanship, and graceful lines, a growing movement to bring it into a fresher, more relaxed realm is well under way.

In this new mode of traditional decorating, fabric color and texture are less formal, albeit no less elegant, and infused with brighter color palettes and less-structured prints. At the same time, wood furniture and finishes are mixed and matched less strictly. Old and new are paired side by side without apology. To achieve a traditional look that is fresh and up to the minute, consider the following points.

CHOOSE COLORS WISELY Softer colors impart a more contemporary, relaxed approach to traditional style. If you prefer a more formal traditional palette, select jewel-tone colors with gold and silver accents.

PAIR OLD WITH NEW Antiques and their reproductions can be used together successfully, and are key to achieving the best possible traditional look. Seek out styles and colors that complement existing pieces.

MIX AND MATCH FABRICS AND TEXTURES When selecting upholstery, accent, and drapery fabrics, choose those that work well together, but do not necessarily match. Keep in mind that upholstery fabrics will likely be part of the room for years, so look for those that are both personally pleasing and will not be dated quickly. Another option is to look for slipcovers for pieces you love but with upholstery that is dated or in poor condition.

ACCESSORIZE, BUT AVOID CLUTTER Today's most successful and elegant traditional interiors keep accessories to a minimum. Keep classic accessories, but don't add too many.

ADD A LITTLE DETAIL Nailheads on upholstered furniture pieces, unique lighting, and unexpected architectural elements such as ironwork and ceiling treatments bring personality to a traditional space. Highlighting these special touches creates

LEFT While the furniture lines in this living room are traditional, the area rug, simple wall color, and lively fabrics give the space a fresh look.

TOP RIGHT Dark hardwood floors and plantation shutters set the tone for this condo's traditional great room. Reflective elements, such as the glass tabletops, and an understated tile fireplace keep the room fresh and interesting.

BOTTOM RIGHT The traditional bones of this living room are complemented by geometric area rug patterns and contemporary lighting.

a sense of warmth within the room and reflects the homeowner's attention to detail.

TRY AN ECLECTIC TAKE ON TRADITIONAL Every piece of furniture in a room does not have to suit a classic traditional vein. Many traditional interior spaces showcase an element from a different genre, including contemporary art.

TOP A minimum number of accessories combined with a neutral yet warm color palette fills this room with light and sets the stage for the un-expected elements of animal prints and a furry rug underfoot.

BOTTOM LEFT Simple yet graphic defines this hallway. The clean interior lines and lack of clutter and fuss are the perfect backdrop for the large-scale contemporary artwork.

BOTTOM RIGHT Monochromatic art-work and matching wall color and fabrics create a sense of serenity in this modern dining room. The warm tones of the traditional dining table anchor the space and keep it from feeling cold.

RIGHT Strong angles, straight-line architec-ture, and a minimum number of accessories give this entry and kitchen a modern vibe. Pops of color provided by the art reflect the homeowner's travels and pique the visitor's curiosity.

Modern Flair

When people hear the term "modern," they often think "cold." And although they want a modern environment, they still want a space that is warm and inviting. Fortunately, a streamlined modern interior can also be luxurious and inviting, layered with classic ele-ments and full of texture and interest. If modern seems too broad a decorating concept, remember that specific styles such as art deco, retro, minimalist, and contemporary can be considered modern style.

A classic modern design is often as much sculptural as it is functional. Monochromatic walls and architecturally clean lines encourage an overall sense of simplicity and orderliness. Furniture lines are often strong and clean, with little or no ornamentation, and a sculptural piece, such as a chair, may be the starting point for the space. Deep wood tones and rich textured fabrics add contrast. Contemporary elements work so well with today's casual, more eclectic direction that the overall feel is comfortable and uncomplicated.

These strong, simple lines offer the perfect backdrop for dramatic art and accent pieces. In this environment, lighting becomes a structural element. The result provides a feeling of harmony throughout the home. To keep the simplicity from becoming sterile, though, look for ways to incorporate other elements into the space.

MIX IN TRADITIONAL ELEMENTS The clean lines and simple styling of modern design don't mean that there isn't room for unexpected traditional "pops."

Traditional patterns and materials can mix easily with sleek finishes and modern accents, and keep the space warm and familiar.

KEEP THE SPACE INVITING Even in a strongly modern interior, the mood can be warm and even romantic. The secret is using texture and contrast. A dark, almost monochromatic palette can set the tone, adding a sense of richness. Hard-edged metals and sleek veneers can be softened by leathers and luxurious fabrics.

INCLUDE SOME SHINE Deep-toned rooms can come to life with shine: The glimmer and reflection of glass and metal on furniture can add this spark of interest. You can achieve this effect by using a series of mirrors as well.

ADD ACCESSORIES Modern does not have to mean bare. You can make any space personal with books, art, and family photographs. The trick is to add personality without creating clutter.

KEEP FUNCTION AND COMFORT IN MIND A modern style is a functional style. Deep-seated upholstery pieces, luxurious fabrics, well-placed lighting, and other accoutrements of comfort and enjoyment can be included in a modern design.

THINK ABOUT THE LIGHT Modern lighting features incorporate both shine and rich wood tones. Metals, such as brushed steel, evoke a sense of the contemporary. The quieter sheens of polished wood and leather can be reflected in the warm glow of candlelight.

OPPOSITE PAGE, LEFT The repetition of graphic elements in the rug design and mirror art in this space emphasizes the overall modern style. Sleek furnishings and an understated paint palette further the contemporary edge.

OPPOSITE PAGE, RIGHT Using mirrors to add shine and reflect light is key in modern design.

TOP RIGHT Metallic-toned paint lends a modern vibe to once-ordinary traditional pieces. Mirrors echo the paint's reflective qualities.

BOTTOM RIGHT Lacquered cabinetry and Lucite furnishings add a modern flair to a traditional space. Colorful accessories and artwork accentuate the modern look.

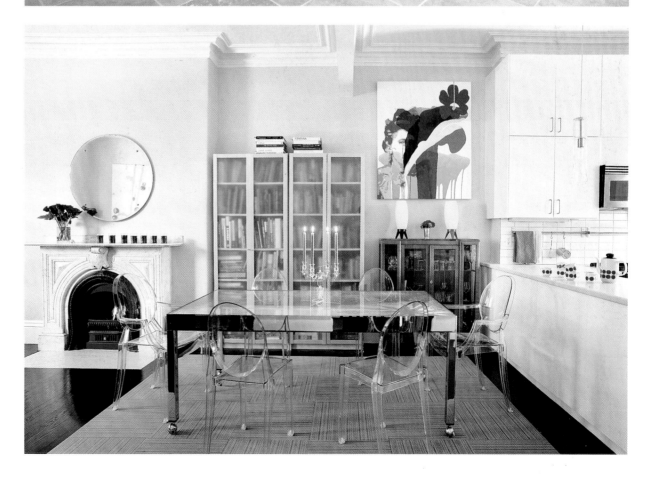

Transitional Blend

Transitional style is a marriage of traditional and contemporary furniture, finishes, materials, and fabrics. The result is an elegant, enduring design that is both comfortable and classic. Because of their simple designs, Asian, Shaker, and Mission-style furnishings are excellent choices for transitional design.

Whereas traditional and modern schemes may introduce a few opposing elements in their designs, the majority of the design elements will be representative of the chosen style. In contrast, transitional style strikes the perfect balance between the two. Through its simple lines, neutral color schemes, and use of light and warmth, transitional style joins the best of both the traditional and modern worlds.

The lines of transitional furniture are typically straight, though the occasional soft, sweeping curve may be thrown in for good measure. This furniture style creates a room that is not too manly and not too frilly, making it comfortable for all. An emphasis is placed on moderately scaled pieces that exude an unassuming, refined style.

Color palettes are very subtle, with an emphasis on ivory, beige, and tan, creating a scheme that is relaxing and uncomplicated. Warm brown to chocolate wood tones are typically the only deep tones used.

With transitional design, flooring is neutral; soft-colored carpets or wood floors in warm tones are generally used. Window treatments are most often modest, solid-color drapes that are shirred onto unadorned metal or wood rods. When blinds or shades are used, they are either clean-line Roman shades or texture-rich woven-wood blinds.

OPPOSITE PAGE, TOP Woven furnishings and wall tapestries provide softness and texture that offset the harder sleekness of the glass and straight-line furnishings. A simple color scheme unifies the two.

OPPOSITE PAGE, MIDDLE This inviting space is perfect for a world traveler. The neutral wall color serves as the backdrop that ties together the disparate treasures on display.

OPPOSITE PAGE, BOTTOM Neutral tones and non-patterned fabrics create a sense of comfort in transitional spaces. Window coverings don't have as much importance as window styling in this family room.

TOP RIGHT Harmonious shades of color ranging from cream to chocolate brown impart a soothing calmness to this bedroom. Rattan elements add an informal note, but still complement the overall color scheme.

BOTTOM RIGHT It's the mix of textures, including a concrete wall and a wooden ceiling, that provides the interest in this room's composition, which blends traditional furniture with a modern flair. Light from the wall of windows offsets the dark furniture and flooring.

ABOVE Simple sconce lighting, a neutral palette, and a pop of greenery add modern elements to what would otherwise be a traditional bathroom design.

OPPOSITE PAGE, TOP LEFT A signature furniture piece or heirloom accented with a blend of contemporary and traditional accessories suits any transitional decor.

OPPOSITE PAGE, TOP RIGHT Natural elements such as stone, granite, and wood are good choices for transitional design because they can play a significant role in both traditional and contemporary schemes.

OPPOSITE PAGE, BOTTOM This mantel setup begins with the traditional look of a mirror and sconce lighting. The accessories, including a row of individual vases and two white mini-pumpkins perched on the end, make it modern.

CHOOSE FABRICS WISELY

The straightforward fabrics used in transitional interior design make up for their lack of color with an abundance of texture and pattern. The texture combinations can range from uneven to smooth fabrics, with most rooms receiving a balanced mixture of several textures. Patterns are usually tone-on-tone designs or small-scale graphic elements.

LOOK FOR CARPETS WITH TEXTURE

Because flooring is neutral, the texture in the carpets or rugs is important. Berber carpets and sisal rugs are popular choices for a transitional blend of styles.

KEEP ACCESSORIES SIMPLE

Tasteful signature pieces are displayed without much fanfare. Try using a single dramatic floral stem or leaf in a chunky modern glass vase. Display artwork and photos in an understated way, with basic white mats and simple frames with clean lines. The metal of choice, for frames as well as for accessories and fixtures, is brushed nickel or silver.

Elements of Design

It's the cabinet layout that gives this kitchen its symmetry. Choosing similar blonde tones for the paint, flooring, and furnishings brings welcome harmony to the space.

No matter which style you prefer, understanding basic design principles will help you create a space that is welcoming and relaxing, but that also will catch and hold your attention. These principles include balance, scale and proportion, rhythm, emphasis, and harmony.

Some people understand balance—using symmetry to lend a gracious feel to a space and then throwing things off with exactly the right asymmetry, just enough to keep things interesting. Others know instinctively about scale and proportion. Still others seem to be able to create a sense of rhythm or to choose just the right focal points to add emphasis to parts of the space. When these elements of design—balance, scale and proportion, rhythm, and emphasis—work together seamlessly, then there is harmony in the room. And a harmonious room is one that is inviting and comfortable—in other words, the best kind of room to be in.

Balance

Balance is achieved in a room when there is visual equilibrium. To accomplish it, you need to think about visual weight. This is not the physical weight of each object in the room, but rather your perception of their weight. For example, dark, warm, intense colors seem heavier than light, cool, low-intensity colors. Opaque materials appear heavier than transparent or translucent ones. Intricate patterns seem heavier than simpler ones.

There are three types of balance: symmetrical, asymmetrical, and radially symmetrical. Symmetry is achieved when you have matching items on each side of a central point. Few rooms are completely symmetrical, but the elements within a room can be. Imagine a fireplace with an identical armchair on either side, a mirror centered directly over the mantel, and candlesticks or family photos in matching frames on both ends of the mantel. Symmetrical balance is pleasing to the eye because it is orderly and restful.

Asymmetry occurs when balance is achieved with objects of different weights. Imagine the same fireplace described above, but this time with two armchairs on one side and a sofa on the other. As another option, the mantel may be arrayed with the family photographs on just one end.

Radial symmetry occurs when objects are placed around a center point. A good example is a round coffee table surrounded by curved sofas or a round dining table with a round chandelier above.

TOP Although this family room layout exemplifies symmetry, there's a subtle touch of asymmetry in the arrangement of accessories above the fireplace.

MIDDLE Radial symmetry is established by a round table and chairs, just like the spokes of a wheel.

BOTTOM The shoji screen, set off to one side, adds an asymmetrical touch to this home office.

Scale and Proportion

Scale is the size of an object or element in relation to other objects in the room. For design purposes, scale is generally labeled as small, medium, or large. Large-scale items need to be matched with small-scale pieces for balance, and vice versa. Most rooms look best when objects and furnishings vary in scale.

When you consider scale, the size of the room and its structural elements should also come into play. A room looks harmonious when objects and patterns are in proportion to one another and to the size of the room. A small room furnished with delicate furniture will have a pleasing look because the scale of the furniture echoes that of the room. A large living room with oversize windows and a sweeping archway that leads to a dining room needs fabrics and furniture that stand up to the drama of the architecture.

ABOVE LEFT Paint can be used to highlight or downplay a room's structural elements. Contrasting paint reveals the architectural lines of the room and creates an eye-catching asymmetrical space.

ABOVE RIGHT A hanging screen of large circles is the right scale for the furniture in the two rooms it divides, giving the entire area an overall sense of correct proportions.

Simple large-scale art provides drama and weight in this dining area, proving that creating impact doesn't have to be complicated.

Rhythm

Rhythm in a room serves much the same purpose as rhythm in music—it creates liveliness in a room just as it gets our toes tapping in a song. Rhythm is achieved by bringing about a feeling of movement in the room. Repetition of objects, colors, shapes, or textures is the most common way to make it happen. For example, repeating bright blue accents—several pieces of blue pottery on a bookshelf, blue pillows on the sofa, and a blue lamp shade—in a pale yellow room keeps the eye moving around the space and establishes a rhythm.

Repeated elements in a range of sizes, such as pieces of pottery with the same shapes or colors, also create rhythm and a feeling of movement. Curved lines that show up in a room's furniture, architecture, and fabric instill movement, as do strong straight or diagonal lines. The way furniture is arranged can also create a sense of motion if the eye is led from one area to another.

Variety is necessary for rhythm, too. Repeated elements should share a common trait, such as color or line, but they should also be different enough to create visual interest. One of the best ways to accomplish this is to present items going from small to large. Imagine a collection of framed rectangular pictures arranged from short to tall atop a piano, with the shorter ones in front and the larger in back. The shape is always the same, but the difference in size and placement creates variety.

OPPOSITE PAGE, TOP LEFT The matching patina on the three sets of closet doors, coupled with the painted casings, provides a strong repetitive accent on this master-bedroom wall.

OPPOSITE PAGE, TOP RIGHT Checkerboard tile provides the beat and sense of energy that may even make doing laundry fun.

OPPOSITE PAGE, BOTTOM Instead of a large transom window, a series of smaller windows repeated along the walls gives more rhythm to the space. The one large window keeps the scheme from being too repetitive.

ABOVE The powerful diagonal lines of this staircase create a sense of movement and rhythm. Contrasting wall colors further emphasize this effect.

Emphasis

Emphasis is defined as giving more significance or presence to some elements in a design than to others, creating a focal point. The focal point in a room can be part of its structure, such as a large stone fireplace. Or it can be something you bring into the room—a favorite painting or a large dining table. A focal point can also be a group of objects—for example, a series of framed prints or an art collection. Color can create a focal point as well. A bright, intense color on the walls or on furnishings will emphasize them more.

When you have chosen a focal point, play it up. Dress large windows with beautiful views with equally beautiful window treatments. Re-cover a favorite chair or sofa in a striking material. Use lighting to highlight a favorite accessory.

Of course, as you emphasize one area, other areas become less important. If your sofa or fireplace is the focal point, then the flooring and wall covering should be subordinate. For a room to be appealing, you need to create a focal point but also places for the eye to rest.

Harmony

Harmony in a room is sensed intuitively. Both unity and variety come into play. Unity means that there are enough similarities in a room's elements to make them look pleasing together, while variety means that there are enough differences in those elements to create interest. Too much unity makes a room boring, while too much variety makes a room appear to be in disarray.

If a neutral color unifies a room, for example, you need variety in the textures of the materials and in the shape and design of the furnishings. If, instead, there is a mix of colors, then the furnishings will look best if the textures and shapes are the same or similar.

TOP The wall color, pattern, furniture placement, and welcoming French doors all work to draw music lovers to this piano room.

BOTTOM Bold color flanked by mirrors directs your eye to the simple headboard in this bedroom.

OPPOSITE PAGE, TOP LEFT Fireplaces are an obvious focal point. However, the color and finish on this one provide added emphasis.

OPPOSITE PAGE, TOP RIGHT Unique structural lines, color, and directional cues turn this space into a power powder room.

OPPOSITE PAGE, BOTTOM The appliances in this kitchen beg for attention with their sleek finishes and vibrant colors. The colors don't overwhelm; there's just enough to add a bit of drama.

Evaluating the Space

Chairs flank the focal point of the room, the fireplace, but don't overwhelm it. Mixing colors and styles and adding favorite mementos to the shelves gives the space a personal touch.

Before you rush out to buy paint and furniture, take some time to evaluate your space and plan your changes. Decide what you want the space to be and how it will function. Look at both the pluses and challenges of the area. There are no hard-and-fast rules for where to begin and what to look at, but the Room Function Checklist at right will give you a start.

Once you've decided what you want, collect color chips, material swatches, and photos of rooms you like. Also, take

accurate measurements of the room itself as well as the spaces available for furniture. These will serve as wonderful tools when shopping.

Keep in mind that you don't need to decorate your home all at once and that it doesn't require a big checkbook. It is more about deciding which changes will deliver the biggest impact and bring you the most joy versus which changes can wait. Shoot for the moon and put your vision on paper. From there, divide the changes into projects that can be tackled in

An unexpected bench is a place for quiet reflection for this homeowner.

Room Function Checklist

- ☐ Is it a well-used and casual room for family and friends or a more formal space?
- ☐ Are pets invited to the space?
- ☐ At what time of day is the space used?
- ☐ What activities go on in this room?
- ☐ Who uses the space?
- ☐ What are the views?
- ☐ Are there structural challenges?
- ☐ Will there be any plumbing and/or electrical challenges?
- ☐ What do I like about the existing space? What do I dislike?
- ☐ And, what is the budget?

a day, a week, or a month, and those that will require a long-term plan.

Looking at the big-picture version of your project will keep you on track for your vision regardless of when you tackle each area. It also ensures that you will keep a natural flow throughout your entire home.

You can find inspiration anywhere and everywhere. Think about places where you have felt comfortable and at ease. It might be a friend's house, a hotel, even a restaurant. What

elements of the space created that sense of peace? Was it the aroma of home cooking, the color on the walls, the level of light, the comfort of the furnishings, or the view through the window? Think about how you can incorporate those elements in your design while still creating a space that is uniquely yours.

Don't overlook an important source of inspiration—your own treasures. They might be family keepsakes, items you picked up on travels, even mementos from special times. Think how you can include them and allow them to tell your story.

Deciding on a Plan

A clutter-free space provides the best jumping-off point. Starting with a clean slate will provide inspiration for your wish list.

OPPOSITE PAGE Color and the melding of old and new pieces give this space its individuality.

O nce you've decided on what you want the room to be, start looking at how you can achieve it. A number of steps will help you narrow down your choices.

CREATE A WISH LIST The sky's the limit—on your list, at least—so write down everything you would like to do or redo. Be sure to include furniture, wall coverings, window treatments, flooring, countertops, cabinets, lighting fixtures, accents, and accessories.

ASSESS YOUR SPACE Think about the things you love, the things you must keep, and the things you can't change. For example, you may love the color of the draperies, you know you need to keep the sofa, and you can't change the size of the room (unless you're planning a major renovation).

Then, draw a bird's-eye-view sketch of your room or rooms, including measurements, to help you see the space you have. A sketch done to scale on graph paper is ideal, but you can also draw something as simple as a rectangle to represent a room and connecting rectangles to represent adjoining rooms.

THINK ABOUT YOUR BUDGET Not everything on your wish list may be possible to achieve, so set your goals accordingly. If you're on a limited budget, check those things that will make

INTERIOR DESIGNER
JENNIFER HILGARDNER ON

Shopping

*S*hopping can be made easier by going with a list of desired items for the room. Organize by drawing out a floor plan of the room. Place furniture and larger objects on the plan simply by drawing a box with a label of 'sofa.' Make sure to have dimensions of rooms as well as furniture sizes, quantity, and color to ensure they will fit in your space."

the most difference, such as new wall color and a new dining table; then mark the things you could add later.

CREATE AN IDEA FILE Look through decorating books, magazines, and catalogs. Flag photos and ideas that appeal to you, whether it's an entire room, a fabric, or a vase of flowers. Include family members in the process, because everyone's purpose for a room counts. If you already have something you love, whether it's fabric, a paint color, a rug, or a piece of furniture, be sure to include it.

Once you've looked at what you want, you can make a plan. Look at the room as a whole, then break it into zones for

specific purposes. Look at furniture layout and traffic patterns. This is also a good time to start collecting materials.

Try to avoid the one-thing-at-a-time approach—just looking for the right color tiles for the floor or a specific fabric for a chair. Instead, start everywhere and look at everything. Visit paint stores, fabric stores, lighting centers, home centers, the flea market, Web sites, and interior-design firms—they all hold a wealth of inspiration. Don't be put off by things you don't like; identifying styles you dislike can be equally important. And don't be timid about collecting samples; you can edit later. Your samples might include fabric, paint chips, wallpaper, carpet, wood, stone, and tile.

Chapter 2

Room-by-Room Design

Whether it is a family kitchen, a spa-like bathroom, a state-of-the-art home office, or even a laundry room, the space you create should be welcoming, soothing, and beautiful. The following pages showcase such rooms throughout the house—and some outdoors—and give advice on planning specific spaces to help you visualize what will work well in your home.

Entryways

Light and bright, this uncluttered entry welcomes all who enter. Large area rugs provide a place to take off shoes and an art-like mirror allows residents to check their appearance before greeting guests.

First impressions are lasting impressions. That's why creating a great entryway benefits both you and your guests. Such an entryway is more than a simple doorway; it's the space where the transition is made from the exterior, public world to the interior, private world. The entryway also offers visitors the first view of your home, so its significance is greater than its size. Your entryway should reflect your home's style and create a single point from which all the other rooms flow.

Architecture and architectural elements can help define the area, but they don't stand alone. The decorating choices also play a large role in creating a warm and welcoming feeling. According to architect Clay Aurell, "The entry foyer should lead the individual beyond, to experience the interior architecture. A functional entryway engages as many senses as possible using fountains, lighting, artwork, views beyond, and a connection to the outdoors."

In the aesthetic sense, this means that an entryway should be a place where family members can pause, either before leaving the sanctuary of home or when returning after a day of work or school. It should also have ample room for greeting guests, with space to chat briefly.

In reality, this means that entryways are drop zones. Car keys, purses, grocery bags, and backpacks—not to mention mail, cell phones, and shoes, coats, and scarves—all end up being dropped in this space. Visitors are often squeezed in amid the many everyday items.

Serving as a bridge between private and public spaces, a place to meet guests, and an area for controlling the clutter of everyday life is a lot to ask of one small space. Meeting all these needs without overwhelming either the room or the people in it takes careful planning.

ABOVE Warm wood and translucent etched-glass panels create a sophisticated yet hardworking entry. The stained maple cabinetry includes a closet for coats and a 4-foot-wide bench above a shoe-storage space. A wall-mounted shelf, topped with a mirror, and a bowl for keys are handy at the front door.

RIGHT The front door and sliding glass panel create opposing forms for visual interest.

BELOW This foyer blends formality with practicality. A pair of 48-inch-high partitions separates the living room from the dining room. One side of the hall features a built-in bench; opposite are cubbies for shoes.

Is there a closet for coats, umbrellas, and hats? If not, a row of hooks can make a good stand-in, as can an old-fashioned hall tree. Baskets mounted on the wall or set on the floor can hold scarves, gloves, and hats. A tall canister will keep umbrellas in one spot.

If you ask people to take off their shoes at the door, a chair or bench will be a good landing spot—one with storage space underneath is a good option. In tight spaces, you might look for a stool or an ottoman that can slide away under a console table. For shoe storage, consider cubbies, under-bench storage, or even a set of shelves. A simple metal tray will keep rain- and snow-soaked shoes from ruining the floors beneath.

Keep adjacent rooms in mind when designing this space. The entryway should set the stage for rooms that are immediately visible and establish the flow for the overall home. Color, furniture styling, lighting, and artwork need not be identical, but they should be related.

Once you've taken care of the necessities, add the extras that will make your entry truly yours. A rug will define the space, especially if the entry is part of a larger space such as a living room. A mirror can make the space seem larger, as well as allow a last-minute visual check before heading out the door. An entryway is a great spot for a signature piece of furniture or art, or a series of decorative pieces. Lamps will give the space a warm touch and add needed lighting. Plants and fresh flowers are always a nice touch. When you make this space uniquely yours, you'll enjoy sharing it with all who enter.

OPPOSITE PAGE, LEFT A narrow built-in bench by the door keeps shoes in a neat row. The small stool nearby is handy for putting them on and taking them off.

OPPOSITE PAGE, RIGHT Time-touched wood elements warm this entryway, where guests can set items down and homeowners can display beloved mementos. Drawers provide a concealed area for the keys, gloves, scarves, and mail that accumulate. Unexpected black-painted doors add drama.

RIGHT Soft colors and painted woodwork combine to welcome all guests who enter this space. A built-in bench with peg system provides a spot to hang coats and a place to sit while putting shoes on and pulling them off.

OPPOSITE PAGE
Tucked into a nook, this entry is simple but sufficient, and suits the clean lines of this Cape Cod home.

THIS PAGE, TOP LEFT Accessed from the garage, this mudroom serves as the family entrance to a mountain vacation home. The combination of stone veneer wall, slate floor, and wood accents creates a warm welcome. Hooks on the wall hold bags and other paraphernalia; a basket is a catchall for umbrellas and snowshoes.

TOP RIGHT At the same house, guests use this front entrance. While more formal than the family entrance, a bench, patina light sconces, and a mountain-appropriate print still fit the style of a vacation retreat.

BOTTOM LEFT Durable porcelain tile flooring and built-in cubbies turn this entry into a functional hub for coming and going. The shelving holds everyday items such as towels, hats, and buckets in an appealing display.

BOTTOM RIGHT The interior porch is an entry hall, a nature-viewing platform, and a sitting area.

Living Rooms

Natural light and woven textures add warmth while pops of color and plants provide personality in this airy living room.

ABOVE A hide-covered wall, extra-long seating, and unique lamps, joined together by a neutral color scheme, create a dynamic living space, perfect for one person or groups.

LEFT The fireplace is the centerpiece of this living room. The contrasting wood and wall colors add interest, while the artwork pulls it all together.

RIGHT The space here is small, but the feeling is large. The dark color of the reclaimed wood-plank floors is echoed in the chair and plays off the white walls, ceiling, and loveseat.

The living room of yesterday was a formal space, used only for special occasions. The living room of today is full of life. It's a place where kids can play, naps can be taken, and a cocktail party can be held with equal ease. It's also a tranquil space where family members can gather and engage in quiet pursuits. As a result, the ideal living room is a place where there is a balanced mix of approachable luxury and welcome comfort, a place where family and friends feel at home.

General contractor John Slaughter comments, "Today's living rooms are unlimited in their function. The significant square footage allows families to reflect their personal lifestyle in creating libraries, game rooms, and lounge areas." Because of this, decorating a living room may seem more challenging than decorating other rooms in the house. Not only does the room need to play multiple roles, it is also the most public part of your home, the "face" that it shows to the rest of the world. At the same time, it needs to blend with the private spaces of your home. The living room sets the tone for the rest of the decor in your house.

INTERIOR DESIGNER
KERRIE L. KELLY ON

Planning a Project

Creating a project 'blueprint' that includes colors and concepts will allow you to have a game plan for the space. Even if you cannot put all your ideas into practice at once, you will benefit from considering the big picture and be able to refer to the master plan when the time finally comes."

LEFT A nature-inspired wall graphic in a distinctly modern color and style forms a surprising but effective backdrop for vintage furniture. Floor-to-ceiling windows coupled with floor and table lamps illuminate the space.

BELOW Vibrant tomato bisque–hued plaster turned a white-painted adobe fireplace into the centerpiece of this space.

Creating a Living Space

No matter which style you prefer, there are a number of factors to keep in mind as you design your living room. The goal is to have everything in the space—from the layout to the decorating details—be comfortable and reach out invitingly to both family members and guests.

A good place to start is the color palette. Because the living room is generally the first substantial room you come to in the house, its color palette should set the tones for variations throughout the rest of the house. Color can be used to set the mood and make a room more inviting. Dark walls can be dramatic; light walls will provide a backdrop for furnishings. Color can also unify a room that has many different textures and furnishings.

Think about a focal point. You may have an architectural detail, such as a fireplace, that you can design around. Another possibility is to design around a piece of furniture, whether it's a couch, a table, even a grand piano. Your focal point might also be an object or objects—you can make a personal statement with a family heirloom, a memento from a trip, an antiques-shop or flea-market find, or a favorite painting or other piece of art. Still another choice is simply to put a lovely color on one wall as an accent.

Comfortable, versatile, and generous seating arrangements are key to a truly welcoming living room. In addition to the main conversation area, create secondary seating areas for

TOP RIGHT A tone-on-tone area rug atop the hardwood floor anchors this living room. Cushioned furniture adds comfort; thoughtfully planned storage helps keep things organized.

BOTTOM RIGHT Old and new are mixed to create a simple yet welcoming living room. The original elements include the dark floors and contrasting white moldings; new art and furnishings add a modern touch.

reading, conversation, or playing games. Have tables nearby to accommodate drinks, books, and games.

Place your furniture to allow traffic to flow smoothly into and through the room. And if the room has to do double duty—family-friendly for everyday use and dressed up for guests—you'll want to plan your space so that the room works well for both options. Look for ways to easily rearrange pieces symmetrically for formal occasions from the more relaxed arrangements for casual times. Look for pieces that can serve multiple functions, such as ottomans that can work as cocktail tables or freestanding shelves that can open up to serve as a bar area. If you'll be moving certain pieces a lot, consider adding lockable casters to them.

Pulling It Together

The most satisfying rooms are those that feel cohesive. Soft furnishings, patterns and textures, lighting, technology, and storage all help to make a room more livable.

Soft furnishings include pillows and window treatments. Blending them to match the dominant color scheme of the furniture, floor coverings, and wall colors is soothing to the senses. However, contrasting colors provide strong accents within the room, adding a pop of color and interest. Remember that a mix of patterns and textures, even when the tones are similar, will give the room a sense of rhythm and movement, keeping it from being stale.

RIGHT A sitting area for reading and relaxing pairs comfortable, informal furniture, like the soft green sofa, with modern classics, like the Eames lounge chair in ivory-colored leather.

Good lighting is essential for both day and night—ambient light for conversation and task lighting for reading and other close-in activities. Keep the lighting flexible so that you can alter the mood in the room. That might mean mixing floor and table lamps with recessed lights or placing certain lights on dimmer switches. If you will use the room a lot during daylight hours, make sure the window treatments do not block sunlight. Jennifer Hilgardner recommends that you "use a mix of ambient, task, and accent lighting to delineate zones. Create a plan that allows you to adjust illumination levels from bright to dim to suit the room's needs."

Technology plays an important role in a living room. Although it may or may not be the room where you watch television or need a DVD player, it is most likely a place where you will want to listen to music. Think about placement of audio equipment as well as where you'll keep accessories, including CDs and vinyl.

Well-thought-out storage options contribute to any room's overall look and feel. Because living rooms are more formal than other rooms, storage tends to be hidden. Even in less formal rooms, though, you'll still want some place to stash things when they're not in use. Good choices include cabinets, chests, and armoires that mix well with other furniture within the room. Tuck footstools under console tables and stow floor pillows in chests, pulling them out when you need extra seating. Select fabrics that coordinate with the rest of your home so pieces can be pulled in from other rooms when necessary.

Display Ideas

Displays of treasured and found items bring vibrancy to a home. They give guests a glimpse into your life and remind you of your history. By effectively using shelving, mantels, tables, and wall space, you can display the objects you love most.

A key to successful display is using a common denominator, such as color, a material, a shape, or a theme, to unify the pieces. Grouping elements in odd-numbered groups, usually three to five pieces, creates an eye-pleasing display. Varying the heights of the elements adds interest.

Interior designer Jennifer Hilgardner explains, "You can display collectibles by creating small groupings scattered throughout the room, on tables, shelves, and within shadow boxes; you can frame a letter for display or place items in glass hurricanes or jars. Choose items in the same color family to create unity within the display area. And remember, less is more. Don't clutter your display by trying to showcase everything. Bring out cherished items and rotate every so often. Others will enjoy them more if they aren't overwhelmed by all the other stuff."

Brightly colored ceramics are showcased against a gray wall.

TOP LEFT This living room is a veritable cocktail of pattern and texture. Rugged, sandblasted block walls and rich wood beams and window frames contrast with the smooth glass coffee table, upholstered seating, colorful bolster pillows, and a soft wavy-patterned rug.

BOTTOM LEFT This contemporary space proves that there's no need to be afraid of color. To make it work, the cool blue-gray colors of the fireplace wall tone down the red and yellow throughout.

ABOVE Low-key furnishings and a soothing color palette in this sitting area allow the home's original fireplace to be the focal point.

BELOW Sometimes less is more, as in this simple arrangement of chairs around a fireplace. Recessed shelves let colorful art pieces provide a pop of color.

Family Rooms

A leather sectional and an unobtrusive recliner soften the hard edges of this family room. Paint accents and drapery frame views and add warmth.

Whether you call it a great room, a family room, or a den, it's usually the most lived-in room in any home. Comfortable seating areas are made for relaxed conversation as well as watching television and movies. Tables and chairs are used for both dining and games. By any name, this room is usually the favorite in every home and deserves a warm decorating touch.

Designed to be shared by family and friends, a great room often includes kitchen, dining, and living areas in one open space, so activities flow together naturally. Sometimes a great room boasts a broad expanse of windows with great views or glass doors opening onto a deck or terrace.

Often situated off the kitchen, the family room, the great room's more modest cousin, is a relaxing spot for family members to gather. A den is usually a smaller room, not necessarily near the kitchen, that is also used for family activities. Dens can also serve as a home office, library, dedicated media room, hobby room, or study.

A functional seating area, placed in a U-shaped configuration, encourages conversation. Artifacts from family travels reflect the personalities of those who live here, while the fireplace and television anchor the space.

Putting Together a Family Room

The key to a successful family room design is keeping comfort in mind. This is the room where everyone gathers. Furniture designer Michael Hennessey describes the family room as "a gathering place that embraces family and friends while exuding a relaxed style. The best family rooms communicate warmth and playfulness by starting with good design and a welcoming scale."

Unifying the areas where so many disparate activities take place can be a real decorating challenge. Perhaps the most important consideration, especially in the great room, is how to keep the space's flow while noting separate areas. Subtle changes within the room, whether in color, furniture placement, even area rugs, can help meet this goal.

We all have ideas about what makes the perfect space and how we would like our family to live. As you plan your decor, keep the following factors in mind.

FAMILY Look at your space and think about your family's activities. Do you like to keep an eye on the kids while you

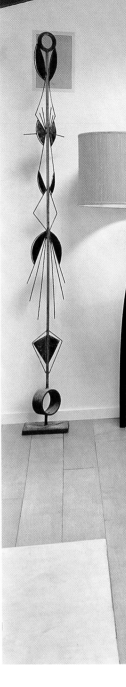

LEFT A neutral microfiber sectional and rugged cocktail table are durable enough for everyday use in this family room. Red and blue accents provided by the area rug and pillow fabrics complement the room; subtle window shades allow sunlight in.

RIGHT This is a room designed for a family, with durable fabrics on the couch and pillows and a bright rug on the floor. A back wall displays collectibles effectively while keeping them out of the main traffic areas.

LEFT A subtly striped rug defines the seating area in this casual living room. Storage cubes with lids that flip to become trays serve as both mobile seating and coffee tables.

are cooking? Do you want to curl up on a window seat to enjoy the view? Do you need space for a desk? Think of all possible uses for the space, then incorporate them into your design.

FURNITURE The furnishings and fabrics in the family room need to be hard-working and durable, with versatile supporting pieces such as side tables and ottomans. They also need to be comfortable and inviting.

MEALS AND ENTERTAINING Many great rooms and family rooms revolve around the kitchen. While cooks generally enjoy being part of the activities and chatting with family and guests, there are practical considerations to keep in mind. Do you want to keep kitchen clutter out of sight, especially during a meal? How can you create a flow that allows the cook, or cooks, to be part of the action but still keeps kitchen pathways clear?

Meals of all sorts will probably be consumed in the family room, so look at ways to incorporate dining options there. Should the dining area be close to the kitchen for convenience or more in the center of the room? Do you want to have a traditional table that can also serve as a homework center, small side tables that can be easily moved around the room as needed, or simply a counter area adjacent to the kitchen?

LIGHTING Daylight that comes through windows, skylights, or glass doors is always welcome, but the real challenge of lighting is after dark. You will want to plan a flexible lighting scheme to divide a large room into several areas and to accommodate a range of activities. Consider overhead lights on a dimmer for eating areas; task lighting for homework spaces, games, and reading areas; and optimal lighting for watching television and movies both during the day and at night.

STORAGE Where family members congregate to read, play games, do homework, watch movies, and listen to music, versatile storage solutions are necessary. Interior designer Jennifer Hilgardner's solution is simple: "Baskets, baskets, baskets—need I say more? Keep children's toys and games under control by having baskets labeled with their names; get them involved by having them create their own labels. Then designate a space for their baskets that is always accessible to them." Other options include cabinets, shelving, and chests.

ABOVE Light colors, soft textures, and elements of nature create a sense of calm in this great room. The high-pitched ceiling gives it a resortlike feeling.

OPPOSITE PAGE, TOP All-white walls and moldings form a neutral backdrop for contemporary furnishings, finishes, and fixtures. The contrast enlivens this comfortable family space.

OPPOSITE PAGE, BOTTOM Cohesive yet playful describes this family space. The couch is a sturdy piece that will last for years; the window treatment, side table, and shag rug add whimsy.

TELEVISIONS AND HOME THEATERS

With the luxury of surround sound, on-demand movies, DVDs, CDs, and gaming systems, we have transformed the way we spend our leisure time. There's no doubt that televisions and home theaters are an important focal point in any family room, but it's also true that most people prefer that they are not the only focal point. As televisions become larger, fitting them into the family room rather than having them overwhelm the space becomes even more important.

Options for minimizing the television's presence are increasingly available and include both off-the-shelf and custom solutions. You can also modify existing pieces, such as cabinets, tables, and armoires. Interior designer Jennifer Hilgardner suggests, "If you don't have an armoire to conceal a television, try placing the television into a niche. Or else choose a TV stand that is the same color as the TV to make them appear as one piece. Use a basket, tray, or wooden box to hold remotes."

It's important to plan for media accessories as well, including sound systems, cable boxes, recorders, and other add-ons. Media specialists can help you plan effectively for housing such gear. General contractor John Slaughter notes, "Homes of today require some thought in placement for media components and surround sound systems. By planning carefully during construction or remodeling, you can place the television inconspicuously, with all of the wiring hidden in the wall."

Finally, let this space reflect the family personality through framed photos and collections—making everyone feel included.

Controlling Media Clutter

Whether you choose to incorporate a media cabinet specifically made to house audiovisual equipment or choose to modify an antique piece, it is easy to make media storage functional and stylish. Storage that is both attractive and inventive is the best solution for clutter-free living. Media collections are notoriously large and are growing larger every day. Employing a portable organization system lets you place items in small containers that you can pull from a shelf without creating clutter. Keep less-used and taller items at the back of shelves and drawers, and favorite, often-used items up front for easy access. Labels and clear containers will allow you to view contents quickly without distracting from the decor.

RIGHT Tapes and DVDs are close at hand yet out of sight in these drawers built into a sofa table.

LEFT A flat-screen television temporarily occupies center stage in this maple storage and display wall. A sliding panel makes it easy to hide the TV when it's not in use.

RIGHT A wall-length shelf is the center of attention here—not the television that its presence helps ground. Pull-out ottomans provide extra seating when it's viewing time.

Dining Rooms

In this modern take on a classic dining room, leather and chrome chairs mix nicely with a deeply grained wooden table and bench. The eggplant-hued wall is both an accent and a backdrop for the art.

Our dining spaces are more inviting and personal than ever. What was once a formally dressed room with fancy place settings is now relaxed and casual. The dining room by nature is a simple space. The centerpiece of any dining room is its table, while the chair choice creates the overall personality of the room. Simply add an overhead light fixture and somewhere to store linens, dishes, serving pieces, and cutlery, and you're ready for family meals or formal entertaining.

Today's dining rooms often serve a variety of functions, including doing homework, paying the bills, or working on a hobby. And in many homes, dining areas are connected to another room, occupying one end of a living room or family room and blending into the larger room. If you want to add formal accents, they'll come from accessories and place settings in lieu of dining furniture or the architecture of the room.

ABOVE A dining area can be small but still have a large impact. Here, the simple shelf also divides the kitchen and family room. The stools can be moved easily to face wherever the action is.

RIGHT Contrasting paint highlights ceiling details and draws attention to a unique dining fixture. Wall-mounted shelving lets family members display their favorite art pieces from travels to the beach. A large mirror adds reflected light to the space.

BELOW A banquette off the kitchen provides plenty of seating as well as hidden storage for linens. Chairs can easily be pulled up to seat even more.

Creating a Gathering Place

No matter how many people are at the table, how simple the meal, or how small the space, you'll want your dining room to be inviting. Choose comfortable furniture that suits your family and arrange it for ease of movement, allowing enough space at the table for each person and enough room around it to serve family and guests gracefully. The table can be against one wall, rather than centered, if the space demands it, and shelves can take the place of a sideboard.

TABLES AND CHAIRS A rectangular table is traditional, but a round one puts everyone on equal footing. For a dual-purpose room, think about two square tables—one for family meals and the other for work or play—that can be joined together for entertaining. And plan for expansion on occasions that call for entertaining more than the regular crew. Comfortable chairs are a must, whether you're serving a quick bite or a multicourse dinner.

STORAGE Rather than the traditional sideboard or credenza, think about open shelving, a rolling cart, or a baker's rack. A shelf mounted at table height or a bookcase that separates the dining area from the living area can provide a surface for serving dishes.

LIGHTING You'll want a light fixture over the table that illuminates the room without creating glare and that complements both diners and place settings. Lighting specialist Zack Rosson suggests, "For a dining space, indirect light is always better than direct. Lamps and candles should be positioned to flatter your guests, and flexibility is a must." You'll need to coordinate the size and placement of the light fixtures with the size of your table. Consider wall sconces to create a soft glow and put lights on a dimmer, if possible.

ACCESSORIES Give the room a personal touch by keeping something on the table when no one is dining; it makes the room look more inviting. Also think about displaying a collection of family china on shelves or favorite artwork on the walls. Trust your own style. If your dining room makes you happy, chances are that guests will be happy, too.

ABOVE A hide rug adds softness to this otherwise contemporary space. Dual dining areas provide space for both quick snacks and more formal meals.

OPPOSITE PAGE, TOP LEFT A contemporary glass dining table lets diners view the handsome traditional rug beneath it.

OPPOSITE PAGE, TOP RIGHT A table pulled up to a window seat creates a cozy dining niche for friends and family.

OPPOSITE PAGE, BOTTOM A custom banquette with colorful throw pillows creates a beautiful morning coffee space or cozy area to play games and complete homework.

Kitchens

There's a reason the kitchen is called the heart of the home: It's where you and your family gather to cook, to eat, to socialize, and, sometimes, just to catch up over a quick snack or a cup of coffee. In many homes, the kitchen has evolved into an all-purpose room, including a dining table, computer desk, entertainment area, even a fireplace.

Today's kitchens are practical, welcoming, and fun. They feature sophisticated colors and innovative components. They also look more like the rest of the house, complete with furniture-like cabinets, wood flooring, and artwork.

The perfect recipe for a beautiful kitchen calls for giving a lot of thought to both the components and the activities that take place in the room, from cooking and cleanup to snacking and socializing. Architect Clay Aurell says, "Kitchens should function well for everyone to enjoy the space, whether cooking, eating, or simply standing nearby. Great design in a kitchen will provide ample prep surfaces while still keeping the necessities in accessible reach." Above all, the perfect kitchen is both comfortable and a pleasure to work in.

LEFT The elements of this open kitchen and dining room run the gamut from traditional cabinets to contemporary seating to industrial lighting. It's the red wall that adds warmth and ties the space together.

TOP RIGHT Dramatic, shiny chocolate subway tiles set the tone in this kitchen, designed for both cooking and entertaining.

RIGHT Dining can be formal or informal in this space: Two eating areas give you the options. The drum lighting creates visual consistency.

BOTTOM RIGHT Vintage style does not need to feel old. This kitchen has a clean and modern feeling even with its traditional features.

Start by defining how the space will work. Do you want an open floor plan or would you rather have separation between the cooking space and the entertaining and eating areas? Do you need storage space, such as a pantry? How about other features, such as a second prep sink, a baking center, or a desk?

Next, consider what the space should look like. Even with the simplest kitchen, you'll need to decide on cabinets, counters, appliances, and flooring. Beyond that, you'll need to determine finishing touches, such as paint and wall coverings, window coverings, and accessories.

Style

The design of your kitchen may be country or contemporary, casual or formal, high-tech or homey—whatever reflects your style preference. Because the cabinets, countertops, and appliances comprise the major components in a kitchen space, you'll want to decide what your overall style will be before choosing them. If you're worried about combining looks with practicality, many designs strive to blend traditional looks with modern conveniences. Architect Clay Aurell notes, "A generously proportioned kitchen with classic materials and up-to-date amenities proves to be both stylish and practical."

Layout

Kitchen layout studies in the 1950s introduced the term work triangle, whose three legs connect the refrigerator, sink, and range or cooktop. An efficient work triangle reduces the steps a cook must take during meal preparation and, whenever possible, is not interrupted by traffic flow.

Today, the work triangle is being challenged by other options; nevertheless, it is still a valuable starting point for good kitchen design. If your space is small, you might want to consider a one-wall kitchen or a galley kitchen. Gaining in popularity are minimalist kitchens, in which obvious kitchen elements such as the refrigerator and upper cabinets are downplayed or tucked out of sight and the kitchen area has the same sensibility as the living space it has merged with. Deluxe kitchens are expansive spaces that often have two or more work zones. Whether your kitchen is large or small, general contractor John Slaughter suggests, "The introduction of an island is an efficient way to add storage and work surface to a kitchen. If the island can house a sink or cooktop, it can

ABOVE This gallery-style kitchen packs function into a narrow space. Bright colors used on the backsplash and rug give it some personality.

ARCHITECT
CLAY AURELL ON

Cabinets

Consider shallow drawers under appliances to maximize storage. Tuck one under a stove to corral baking sheets and tins. Toe-kick drawers can be installed to capitalize on space under almost any cabinet."

tighten the work triangle and save steps in the kitchen."

Cabinets

Your first decision is whether to keep your existing cabinets, perhaps refinishing or refacing them, or to replace them. If you replace them, you will need to decide if you want "fitted" or "unfitted" cabinets. A fitted kitchen, the almost universal choice since the mid–20th century, consists of banks of matching upper and lower cabinets with the appliances incorporated into them. "Unfitted" kitchens generally have a mix of styles and colors. The cabinets are more furniture-like. Upper cabinets may float singly on the wall or may sit on the countertop like a hutch; shelves may take the place of cabinets.

Other decisions include cabinet construction and style and whether you want stock, semicustom, or custom cabinetry. You'll also want to decide on the materials and finishes. You can always mix things up, choosing different materials and complementary ones, to bring personal style to your kitchen.

TOP There's no doubt that this is a contemporary kitchen. From the stainless steel appliances to the frosted-glass cabinets, the sleek black counters, and the vivid (and futuristic) tomato-red stools, everything is designed to say "now."

MIDDLE Glazed furniture-like cabinetry lets this kitchen fit in with the other rooms in the house.

BOTTOM Mixing lower stainless steel cabinets with upper beadboard cabinets is unusual but effective. The neutral tones of gray and white allow the vintage-style turquoise stove to stand out.

Countertops

These are the workhorses of the kitchen and need to stand up to a lot of wear and tear. Beyond each surface's aesthetic appeal, you want to weigh its physical characteristics. You want countertops that are water-resistant, durable, and easy to maintain. Before deciding, consider how you will use the countertops. Do you want surfaces for chopping or placing hot pans? Do you mind sealing surfaces? Will blemishes bother you or do you need a surface that won't show fingerprints and water spots?

You needn't limit yourself to one type of material. Granite may be your choice for the perimeter countertops while butcher block may be what you want on a prep island. Tile and flooring specialist Heather Loehr suggests, "Add a marble countertop to the island if this is a prep area. It's a great working space for a family member who loves baking because of its functionality. You can roll out the cookie dough on the marble, but the marble surface looks great when not in use."

Backsplashes are another consideration. The most basic is a simple curb a few inches tall that is either part of the countertop or a separate strip of material. A more common backsplash runs from the countertop to the bottom of the upper cabinets or windows. A full-wall backsplash runs from the countertop to the ceiling. Backsplashes can either match the countertop material or contrast with it. Ceramic tile has long been the most popular choice, but well-sealed wood, stainless steel, glass tile,

LEFT A black solid-surface countertop ties the stainless steel gas stove and dishwasher to the bright white cabinets. The faucet set at an angle adds interest.

RIGHT Unexpected pendant lighting, warm woods, and a rug runner soften the effect of the stainless steel appliances and concrete countertop.

mosaics, and stone are becoming more common.

Appliances

These include the standard refrigerator, stove, and dishwasher; you may also want to look at cooktops, combination ovens, wine coolers, warming doors, and much more. The trick is to figure out just what you need.

REFRIGERATORS Full-size refrigerators come in a variety of styles, including top-mount freezers, bottom-mount freezers, side-by-sides, and those with French doors. Additional choices include color, finish material, door finishing options (from solid to glass to panels that match the cabinetry), handle styles, and extras such as filtered water and an icemaker. Other refrigeration options include mini-fridges and wine coolers. A new development is refrigerated drawers, designed to stack on top of one another and fit under a counter.

RANGES, COOKTOPS, AND OVENS

The standard range has four burners and an oven. Beyond the basic model, ranges can feature up to eight burners, a grill, and more than one oven chamber. Professional ranges are showing up in more and more kitchens, as are vintage styles, whether original older stoves or new ranges designed to look old.

Separate cooktops work well built into islands and on peninsulas, and the sepa-ration allows several people to work in the kitchen at the same time. Wall ovens can be easily worked into a floor plan. Multiple wall ovens can be stacked on top of one another and, because they are built into the cabinetry, they can be positioned at any height.

Microwaves and toaster ovens are considered essential in today's kitchens. Consider mounting a microwave over the range or into the cabinets to free up counter space. Small convection ovens are gaining in popularity, as are warming drawers.

Whether you've opted for a range or a cooktop, ventilation will be required. Hoods are popular, but you can also find cabinet undermount ventilation systems, combination microwave ventilation systems, and downdraft vents. Be sure to factor in how noisy a ventilation system is. Also, be sure the hood size will match your stove's heating capacity.

DISHWASHERS Today's dishwashers are much more energy efficient and much quieter than past models. The standard dishwasher is still the full-size undercounter option. These offer a range of design and cycle possibilities, and come in a variety of finishes. Dishwasher drawers are a new and popular option. You can run each drawer separately, so you can feel good washing just one drawer's worth of dishes.

SINKS AND FAUCETS A sink is the one kitchen feature you're sure to use daily. It's also highly visible, so choosing a style and material is a personal and important decision. The basic styles are drop-in (or overmount), undermount, integrated, and apron. You will need to decide on material, whether it's enameled cast iron, stainless steel, or another material, and whether you want a large single basin or a sink that's divided into two (or more) bowls. You may also opt for a separate prep sink.

Faucet choices seem endless, but your faucet needs to work with your sink, both as an aesthetic element and practically, so that it fits into the available cutouts. Gooseneck and tall faucets work well with tall pots. Many faucets feature pullout sprayers. Other options include purified-water taps that provide instant chilled or hot water, built-in soap dispensers, and pot fillers.

Flooring

Every kitchen deserves a floor that is beautiful. But in addition, a kitchen floor needs to be comfortable underfoot, watertight, slip-resistant, hard to damage, and easy to clean.

Flooring also needs to work well with the other design elements in your room. Traditional options include vinyl, linoleum, wood, stone, and ceramic tile. Newer options include laminate flooring, cork, bamboo, and concrete.

OPPOSITE PAGE, TOP LEFT A dual sink with a tall faucet is a practical choice for most kitchens.

OPPOSITE PAGE, TOP RIGHT Red undermount sinks enliven the quiet gray-green of the countertops.

OPPOSITE PAGE, BOTTOM The prep sink in the corner of the island is accessible to anyone working at the island or the stove. The second sink is wide and deep for serious cleanup.

TOP RIGHT Both can lighting and pendants are on dimmers to set the mood for the large eat-in kitchen.

BOTTOM RIGHT An ornate metal chandelier is the perfect accessory for this rustic eat-in kitchen.

Lighting

A kitchen may be efficient and good looking, but with poor lighting, it will be an unpleasant and tiring place to work. You need shadowless illumination for the entire room as well as bright light for specific tasks. Built-in uplights over the cabinets can provide ambient light; those under the cabinets can provide needed task lighting. With multiple sources and dimmer controls, you can have bright light for working and soft light for atmosphere.

While kitchen lighting has traditionally consisted of ceiling lights or recessed fixtures, pendant lamps and chandeliers are becoming increasingly popular. Depending on the size of your space, you may want a mix of fixtures—and switches. Lighting specialist Zack Rosson says, "The kitchen requires plenty of ambient and task lighting. Work surfaces need lighting without glare. Recessed can lights combined with halogen or fluorescent under-cabinet lighting is great, but for added style and light, introduce pendant lights over an island-type area."

Storage and Display

The cabinet is the old standby for kitchen storage, but other options abound. Hutches and armoires are making a comeback in kitchens, as are islands, carts, racks, and shelves.

Pantries are making a comeback too. Food pantries, whether walk-in rooms or simply a wall cabinet or closet, are ideal for canned goods and paper products as well as less frequently used small appliances. The traditional butler's pantry is a walk-through space between the kitchen and the dining room, designed to hold dishes, glassware, linens, silver, and candles; it may also include a sink.

Open storage is also becoming popular, and works well in both traditional farmhouse kitchens and contemporary styles. Open storage options include built-in shelving, open shelves, plate and pot racks, wine and spice racks, tables, and carts.

Closed storage options, which keep kitchens from looking overly crowded or messy, include appliance garages, drawers, and pullouts. Freestanding furniture may offer either open or closed storage, or a combination of the two.

As the kitchen has become a central meeting place for family and friends, presentation has become a priority for many homeowners. It is now fashionable to display almost everything in the kitchen—from dishes to pots and pans to gourmet oils and vinegars. Cabinetmakers and storage manufacturers have risen to the trend with attractive display cases, baskets, canisters, and racks. Other options include open shelves and glass-doored cabinets.

Vintage tableware is handy as can be while showing off the homeowner's collection and enlivening the room.

LIGHTING SPECIALIST
ZACK ROSSON ON

Small Changes

Sometimes even a small change will make a huge impact. Try updating light fixtures. Simply add dramatic glass pendants over the kitchen island. This provides the task lighting that is needed while adding visual interest."

Finishing Touches

Once you determine the main elements of the kitchen, it's time to think of the finishing touches. These include window styles and treatments, wall treatments, seating, and decorative accents.

The windows in your kitchen should match the style of the space, whether they're multipaned traditional windows or single-paned contemporary styles. In either case, look for windows that are energy efficient. When it comes to window coverings in kitchens, less is often better than more. Because kitchens often don't need to provide the privacy that other rooms do, you can even go without window treatments altogether. However, valances or simple shades will add color and texture without over-whelming the space. Look for easy-care fabrics or non-fabric options such as wood blinds.

Kitchen walls have to stand up to humidity and grease as well as everyday dirt and fingerprints. Because of this, painted walls are often best. Choose a paint that's easy to clean, such as semi-gloss or eggshell. If you prefer wallpaper, look for one that is both durable and easy to wipe clean. For an easy-clean surface that's handy for messages and notes, use chalkboard paint on a wall, door, or cabinet.

A place to sit in the kitchen is a plus, whether for eating, preparing food, or simply chatting with the cook. Barstools can be pulled up to islands and counters, and are a good choice for limited space. Tables and chairs require more space; be sure there's enough room to walk around a table or pull out the chairs. If you have a nook or a bump-out, consider adding bench seating. For the ultimate in relaxing comfort, you can always add a sofa to the space.

When it comes to choosing stools or a table and chairs, take the same approach as you did in the rest of the house,

whether that means sleek and contemporary, traditional styling, or an eclectic mix. Keep cleanup in mind when choosing materials; both upholstery and table surfaces should be easy to clean.

For most people, the kitchen is the hub around which family and friends revolve. It makes sense that the decor reflects the dwellers' tastes and interests. Decorative accents give any kitchen a personal touch. These include such practical pieces as rugs and furniture or individual items such as decorative plates, cookbook libraries, candles, or pottery collections. Artwork adds interest to a kitchen space, but be sure that it can be easily cleaned. Mounting a magnetic board between cabinets can be an alternative to covering the refrigerator door as well as a display spot for the week's menu and schedule. Adding coordinating table linens will round out the space. Introducing family photos and treasures can add whimsy and character as well.

Going Green

Remodeling a kitchen offers a number of options for choosing sustainable materials. If you're refacing existing cabinets, look for sustainably harvested veneers; if repainting, look for low- or no-VOC (volatile organic compound) paints. If you're buying new cabinets, pay attention to what they're made of; you can find manufacturers that use nontoxic soy-based adhesives instead of formaldehyde. If your cabinets are hardwood, check that the wood is from a certified managed forest; look for the FSC (Forest Stewardship Council) logo.

If you're removing cabinets, consider having them deconstructed or removed without damage. You can then use them in a garage workshop or office, or donate them to a good cause.

A growing number of recycled and "green" options for countertops are available. Check carefully, though, as the benefits and actual "greenness" of the materials may vary. Ask about the life span of the product, whether its content is recycled, and whether the manufacturing process is benign. You can also look for recycled metals. Still, the most environmentally conscious counters are made from natural, renewable materials that are both recyclable and biodegradable, such as wood.

Buying energy-efficient appliances is a smart move. This is increasingly easy to do: The Department of Energy (DOE) sets minimum performance standards and the Federal Trade Commission requires yellow Energy Guide labels on refrigerators and dishwashers, allowing you to compare energy usage. Energy Star models, while more expensive at the outset, will save you money by providing better performance and lower monthly utility bills. Still, all appliances consume energy, so consider carefully the number of them you need.

LEFT Recycled glass embedded in concrete makes a heat-resistant, easy-to-clean, and environmentally friendly countertop.

BELOW A counter of FSC-certified recycled paper in nonpetroleum, nonformaldehyde resin boasts integral color and is heat- and stain-resistant.

OPPOSITE PAGE, TOP LEFT This stylish kitchen features FSC-certified flooring and cabinets, and counters composed of concrete containing rice hulls.

OPPOSITE PAGE, TOP RIGHT This green-built kitchen includes formaldehyde-free wheatboard cabinets, quartz-crystal countertops, and thin-striped bamboo flooring throughout.

OPPOSITE PAGE, BOTTOM In this eco-friendly kitchen, the vivid countertops and backsplash are made of quartz chips in a resin binder. The floor, counter, and buffet are bamboo, and the cabinets are covered in sustainably harvested white fir veneer.

Heart of the Home

Using similar colors in the backsplash and the adjacent wall provides continuity in an open space with a mix of finishes.

OPPOSITE PAGE, TOP The simple earth tones of the paint complement the darker furniture in this room. A coffered ceiling makes sense of unwanted beams and gives an air of formality to the main space.

OPPOSITE PAGE, BOTTOM A variety of finishes keeps the kitchen space interesting. The dark and light woods add an eye-catching element to an otherwise simple spot, and the paneled wall adds storage. Vintage furniture and modern cabinetry blend well.

When designer and architect Heather Wells purchased a loft in Boston's South End neighborhood, the space was a white box with concrete floors and a dated kitchen and bath. Wells wanted to make the most of the 38-foot-long wall of windows and extensive view by keeping the interior as open as possible. The result is a single, flowing space with cooking, eating, relaxing, and bedroom areas still clearly defined.

Mahogany cabinets line the interior walls of both the kitchen and dressing areas while painted lacquer cabinets divide the front hall from the main bedroom. A coffered ceiling defines the living room space, and sheer curtains partition off the bedroom.

The furnishings that Wells chose are primarily contemporary and warm, with New England painted antiques adding an eclectic touch. These pieces include the kitchen island and another farm table that sits beneath the wall-hung television and helps anchor the end wall of the living room. Small antique rugs provide color and comfort.

The Elements

- **Flooring:** Rift and quarter-sawn white oak are finished with a deep walnut brown stain.

- **Cabinets:** Perimeter cabinets feature mahogany veneer stained a dark walnut; floating cabinets with a matte lacquer finish, used as wall dividers and for storage, were custom-painted to match the wall color.

- **Kitchen Island:** A lucky find, a country plant-stand table finished with a lagos azul limestone top, became the kitchen island.

- **Tile and Backsplash:** Lagos azul limestone with a matching curb forms the countertops; teal-colored brick tiles with a crackle glaze serve as the backsplash.

- **Hardware:** Brushed stainless steel bar pulls and knobs are used throughout the kitchen area; the pot filler over the stove, with a brushed nickel finish, coordinates.

- **Appliances:** The integrated dishwasher, refrigerator, and stove hood all feature full overlay panels so that they disappear into the space.

Bedrooms

Today, a bedroom is much more than a place to sleep—it is a multifunctional place to exercise, work, and unwind as well. A well-designed bedroom is the best gift you can give yourself. You spend a third of your life in this space, so choose to invest in quality and comfort.

Because they are private spaces, bedrooms are a true reflection of your personal style. So think about what makes you happy and what speaks to your interests. That knowledge will help you create the bedroom of your dreams.

Bedroom Basics

What do you need in a bedroom? No matter the style or decor, every bedroom should have a comfortable bed, a good reading light, bedside tables, carpeting or rugs, and window treatments that ensure darkness and privacy. Adequate closet and bureau space is a must, so keep in mind your storage needs.

What you choose to put on the walls will help create the room's mood. As interior designer Jennifer Hilgardner says, "The right color can make your bedroom feel like a retreat."

LEFT Simple and serene, with natural light and light color tones, this bedroom is ideal for reading and relaxing as well as getting a good night's sleep.

TOP RIGHT Custom fabrics combine with a rich wall color to add a sense of luxury to this master bedroom, reflecting the owner's style. The area rug is a fun and contrasting accent.

BOTTOM RIGHT Accents of red and gray plus contemporary styling keep this pink-walled sitting area from being overly feminine.

Color can provide a soothing or dramatic backdrop, flowered wallpaper will help bring the garden indoors, and painted stripes lend a tailored look.

Furnish a bedroom with fabrics, scents, textures, and colors that calm. Add character by mixing the wood finishes, combining fabric patterns, or choosing color combinations that are unusual but fit your personal style. Even something as simple as purchasing ready-made drapes and adding a band of custom fabric to the top or bottom will make customize a look.

Such attention to details is what will make the room your own. A comfortable chair for reading, shelves for books, and a fireplace for warmth and romance may be what you want. Or piles of pillows and stylish bed linens may be your choice. Fresh flowers and soothing fragrances will add a welcome touch. Be sure to include a treasured item that has personal meaning for you.

Master Bedrooms

A master bedroom suite, including the bathroom and dressing area, is often large enough for many uses. Your bedroom can be a self-contained space full of amenities, and your favorite place to hang out.

When decorating a master bedroom suite, think about how the rooms flow into one another. Delineate the rooms with distinctive touches, but consider using a similar color in all areas to tie them together and give the space a harmonious look.

Edit your bedroom furniture and accessories so that the area seems more spacious. The goal is to have everything in balance: color, style, and furnishings.

Above all, choose furniture that works for you and your needs, whether it's part of a matched bedroom set or not. Furniture designer Michael Hennessey suggests, "Unmatched furniture pieces are always more interesting. If you need your nightstands to offer storage, try a small-scale dresser or trunk and an oversize round table instead."

Guest Rooms

Guest rooms are typically small and often unused, and may have to share their space for other uses. Still, they should have a definite style and presence. You don't have to splurge, but choose a soothing wall color and comfortable bedding. Be sure there's room for guest clothing—provide both space and extra hangers in the closet—and offer a luggage stand for a suitcase or empty drawers for folded clothes. Added touches include a good reading light, an alarm clock, a water carafe and glass,

OPPOSITE PAGE Monochromatic tones dominate this master bedroom, but color accents and a zebra rug give it unique flair.

ABOVE Buttery walls and cool fabrics combine to create a relaxing space. Unmatched furniture is unexpected, and adds interest.

LEFT Simple details, like flowers, a reading lamp, and a warm throw, can give a guest room a hotel-like feel.

RIGHT Positioning a bed in a corner can add space to any bedroom. Pendant lighting is a surprise design element in this room.

maybe even a robe and slippers. When guests are due, add fresh flowers to the room. Interior designer Jennifer Hilgardner adds, "Small luxuries count for a lot in a guest room. Extra pillows on the bed, candles, books, flowers, even a throw blanket for a cat nap are all thoughtful additions to ensure a welcome visit."

If the guest room is truly a multipurpose space, look for storage options for when guests come to visit. Closed storage, whether it's freestanding furniture or built-ins, can keep daily clutter out of sight. Consider furniture that has multifunctional uses: A furniture-style file cabinet can also work as a side table for a bed; a chest can hold office supplies as well as extra blankets.

INTERIOR DESIGNER
KERRIE L. KELLY ON

Bed Linens

Splurge if you can on high-thread-count sheets, especially in the master bedroom. They will make you feel pampered every day. Add to this soft and luxurious blankets. Finally, complete the space by topping the bed with a down comforter encased in a silk duvet and layering on down sleeping pillows. The result will be the ultimate heavenly bed."

FAR LEFT Artwork becomes a headboard in this comfy bedroom designed to grow with a young girl.

LEFT Easy-to-apply stick-on circles provide instant art in this child's bedroom.

BELOW Playful paint colors and fabrics are more than appropriate for teenagers' rooms. Creative storage solutions help to keep the space tidy.

Children's Rooms

For a child, a bedroom is more than just a place to sleep. It is a place to do schoolwork, listen to music, play games, sprawl on the floor, rough-house, read, build models, daydream, visit with friends, and keep innumerable possessions. You'll need to plan carefully to create a room that serves all those functions, yet is comfortable and inviting—and has enough staying power to require only minimal redecorating every few years.

The ultimate experts on what kids like best are kids themselves. "Have kids feel involved in the design process by letting them help with selections for the room," suggests furniture designer Michael Hennessey. Include children's interests and ask for their opinions as you create a decorating scheme. But don't go overboard: Children's interests change often, so use accessories that can be easily replaced when interest wanes. What you want is a room that both meets your needs and pleases your child.

The furniture and accessories should be appropriate for your child's age, but they should also be adaptable—not trendy. As Hennessey says, "Pick children's furniture that can grow with the child."

Also, plan to provide space for the many activities that may take place in a child's room. This includes space for visiting friends and sleepovers, a place for play (remember to have room for a train set or dollhouse), and a spot with a desk and good light for doing homework.

Children should have a sense of control over their environment. They should be able to hang up clothes, reach toys and books, and sit in chairs that suit their size. An added benefit: They'll learn early that they can do things for themselves.

Incorporate a favorite color into the room somewhere. Fortunately, color, especially on the walls, is easy to change. To personalize a space, consider adding a mural or chalkboard wall. If you can, draw wall art freehand; if you're not artistic, look for stencils or stick-on wall decor. You can also find letters that will let you embellish a wall with sayings that are special to your child.

The younger the child, the more durable and easy to clean the room materials should be. For any child, a safe environment is critical. Review the literature on all surfaces and products, and get up to date on product recalls before you make major purchases.

The Green Bed

You can get a comfortable bed and an environmentally friendly night's sleep with linens, mattresses, and bed frames that are all readily available. Other ways to make your bedroom healthier include opening windows, bringing in houseplants, and leaving shoes outside the bedroom door.

ABOVE LEFT Look for reclaimed or sustainable materials, including bamboo and FSC-certified wood.

ABOVE RIGHT Wool is a natural flame retardant, so mattresses that contain it don't need to be treated with chemical retardants. Other choices include natural latex and organic cotton.

ABOVE LEFT For linens, choose pesticide- and chemical-free fabrics, such as organic cotton.

ABOVE RIGHT Look for natural, untreated fibers like wool or organic cotton, or 100 percent natural latex.

Bathrooms

Crisp white walls, soft aqua accents, and the shimmer of a glass-tile backsplash turn a simple bathroom into a spa-like retreat. The glass wall separating the vanity from the shower keeps the overall space feeling open, light, and airy.

Though not traditionally viewed as the most glamorous room in the home, the bathroom has become a personal oasis—a haven for health, beauty, and general rejuvenation. Privacy, comfort, and a bit of surprise help take a bathroom from simply functional to high design.

Whether you're decorating a small guest bath, a larger family bath, or a luxurious master bath, you'll want to make the space as pleasingly useful as possible. The style you choose for your bathroom will be established, at least in part, by the materials you select. With a wide range of finishes to choose from, including tile, mosaics, and stone, and a huge variety of plumbing and light fixtures, the possibilities are truly endless. Look for ways to integrate distinctive finishes, artificial and natural light, and artwork to bring the space to life.

An important part of any bathroom is privacy, but don't give up an amazing view or any connection to the outdoors, whether it's a window or even a door to a private patio or outdoor shower.

Master Baths

Your master bath might include a walk-in closet or dressing area, a separate shower and tub, plus a water closet. It might even sport enough space for exercise equipment, saunas, and steam showers. Because they don't get as much wear and tear as family bathrooms, master baths are places where you can splurge on materials and finishes. No matter which choices you make, the result should be both soothing and functional.

The style of the bath should coordinate with the rest of your master suite. Choose colors for the walls and floor that match or coordinate with the primary colors of the bedroom. Cabinets, countertops, and light fixtures should reflect the style of the master bedroom as well. Add personal touches through rugs, accessories, and artwork. Plants will add life to the room and, given enough light, thrive in the humidity.

If two people will share the master bath, plan for both togetherness and privacy. Architect Clay Aurell feels that "It is important that both people can use the bathroom at the same time." You may want to add a second sink, create a dressing area, or divide the room into zones for different functions.

TOP The hammered copper tub is the star in this master bath. A custom window treatment and custom art add to the overall sense of luxury.

BOTTOM LEFT A large corner tub surrounded by a soft color palette of blues and greens is a tranquil spot to soak in.

BOTTOM RIGHT A classic tub is tucked into the corner of a master bath for an intimate view of the outdoors.

ARCHITECT
CLAY AURELL ON

Master Baths

If you're designing a new master bath, always have a water closet for the loo, and, if possible, a separate shower and tub or a nicely designed custom tub/shower combo sized for two."

Family Baths

Family baths are shared baths, and, as such, often need to accommodate a number of people at one time. If you have room, add a second sink; using pedestal or wall-hung sinks will create a greater sense of space in a smaller room. You may also want to separate the toilet from the rest of the room, even if it's only with a half wall.

Because these baths are generally stand-alone rooms, you can create a look that is unique. Subdued colors will add a sense of tranquility, often necessary in a busy household; bright colors will make the space lively and cheerful. Be sure to add lots of storage, whether through vanities, cabinets, shelving, or racks and baskets. Also include plenty of space for hanging towels and wet clothes. Finally, choose durable surfaces that are easy to clean.

Kids' Baths

A bathroom just for children is a great choice for a family. Keep this room both cheerful and functional. Pick a theme, then use whimsical tiles and lots of color to make it fun. Add easily accessible storage for bath toys, towels, swim trunks, and other kid necessities. Suddenly it will be a place where children will want to take a bath.

Safety is an important aspect of any bathroom that children use. In addition to the standard measures, such as installing safety latches on doors, putting childproof covers on receptacles, and installing a toilet lid lock, consider adding slip-resistant flooring, choosing a bathtub with a textured surface on the bottom, and creating rounded corners on counters and walls. You can also install scald-free tub and shower valves.

Make sure the surfaces can stand up to plenty of use. Walls, flooring, cabinets, and countertops should be sturdy, long lasting, and easy to clean. Look for faucets that are easy for small hands to operate. Hang towel bars so they are within easy reach, and make sure they're securely attached to a stud so they can't be pulled off the wall.

A big issue in kids' bathrooms is the height of the counter and sink. You have several options. Step stools are an easy addition, though they can get in the way. You can also install lower vanities and shorter toilets, though they may need to be replaced as children grow. The same is true of installing lower showerheads. Another option is to incorporate a stool within the toe-kick of the vanity that can be pulled out when needed and pushed back out of the way when not in use.

ABOVE LEFT This cheerful bath features a corner bench that is a perfect place for getting dressed.

ABOVE RIGHT A stool incorporated into a toe-kick can be pulled out only when needed so you don't keep tripping over it.

Half Baths

Half baths, or powder rooms, are generally small, usually consisting of just a sink and toilet, so it can be hard to fit a lot into them. Yet these rooms can really make a statement.

Because of their small size, these spaces can handle decorating choices that might be overwhelming in a larger space. A half bath is the place for the one-of-a-kind purple sink, the retro Victorian vanity and wallpaper, or sleek modern fixtures.

Because these rooms aren't subjected to as much steam and splashing as regular bathrooms, you can use more water-sensitive materials. Even so, it's still a good idea to add a fan. This will help remove what steam comes from the sink, and the noise will create privacy, especially for rooms near the living areas or kitchen.

Spa Baths

If you can, consider turning your master bathroom into a home spa, creating, as tile specialist Tracy Bowman says, "a tranquil space that nourishes the spirit." The feel of a luxurious retreat can be created by selecting simple plumbing fixtures, materials, and accents drawn from nature.

Start with a soothing color palette, inspired by water, sunlight, or foliage. Windows allow fresh air to circulate, and a view outdoors promotes serenity. Install a luxury bath or steam shower. Wall-mounted sinks open up additional floor space, and sleek cabinetry helps keep the space clean and uncluttered. Luminous glass tiles provide a subtle reflective quality and shimmer, while natural stone adds an organic element to the space.

Incorporate a cozy chair or terry cloth–covered bench in your tranquil space. Put a dimmer switch on the lights and install speakers on either side of the bathroom. Finish the space with plush towels, lotions, and fresh flowers.

TOP LEFT Simple touches, such as crystal knobs and a home for goldfish, turn a bath from ordinary to stylish.

TOP MIDDLE A furniture-style vanity and a candle-like wall sconce give this half bath a sophisticated flair.

TOP RIGHT Petrified-wood tiles that look like stone, white walls, warm-hued wood, and uncovered windows contribute to a simple, nature-inspired aesthetic in this spa-like bath.

BOTTOM LEFT Half baths are a great place to use materials that don't stand up well to lots of moisture, such as this textural grass-cloth made from plant fibers.

BOTTOM RIGHT Dark wood cabinetry, a subtle slate floor, and a luxurious tub and shower combine to form a relaxing retreat.

Nature-Inspired Retreat

The tub, built into a teak shelving system with one large window opening out to the koi ponds, is surrounded by an overspill trough filled with black stones.

OPPOSITE PAGE, LEFT Custom cabinetry is home to a solid-surface top and undermounted sinks for easy cleaning. The textures and colors in the pebble-stone flooring complement the natural elements—inside and outside. Plus, you get a foot massage every time you walk on it with bare feet!

OPPOSITE PAGE, RIGHT Limestone-like tiles and oil-rubbed bronze plumbing fixtures are timeless elements. A teak bench and teak flooring provide comfort.

Architect Clay Aurell created an Indonesian-inspired spa-like retreat to overlook the koi ponds and bamboo gardens in this Japanese-style home in Santa Barbara, California. Nature-inspired elements are used throughout, from the teak and teak veneer on the cabinetry to the pebble-stone tile on the floor. The custom vanity was built to a non-standard depth to fit this smaller space without overwhelming it. The tub faucet, mounted on the side so it's out of the way, gives the tub the look of a fountain. The shower is finished with a teak floor for comfort.

The Elements

■ **Tub:** A contemporary Japanese-style tub includes a handheld showerhead and easy-access controls mounted on the deck.

■ **Tub Faucet:** An oil-rubbed bronze waterfall-style filler provides a fountain-like feel in the tub area.

■ **Cabinetry:** Solid teak combined with teak veneer warms the walls and adds a natural element to the master bath.

■ **Vanity:** A solid-surface engineered-stone countertop enables easy cleanup, under-mounted rectangular sinks mirror the tub, and a raised height accommodates creative storage.

■ **Faucets and Fixtures:** Oil-rubbed bronze faucets and fixtures are easy to use and maintain.

■ **Flooring:** The stone tile used throughout most of the room complements the natural elements. Teak in the shower adds warmth, as does the radiant heating installed beneath the flooring.

■ **Lighting:** Sconces on dimmers allow the homeowners to change the overall mood within the room.

■ **Window:** A picture window that frames the view functions as living art.

Bathroom Basics

No matter what type of bathroom you're designing, there are some basic features to keep in mind. These include cabinets, countertops, tubs and showers, sinks and faucets, and toilets. You'll also want to think about wall and floor coverings, lighting, and additional options.

CABINETS AND COUNTERTOPS These set the style and tone of the room. They need to be beautiful, but at the same time they need to be functional and easy to care for.

There are any number of cabinet options, from stock pieces to semi-custom and custom choices. A new trend is to use a piece of furniture, such as a dresser, dressing table, or bookshelf, in the space in place of traditional vanities.

Pedestal and open vanities add a sense of space and elegance to any bath, but be sure to keep storage needs in mind. You may have to sacrifice some of the openness for space to store toiletries, towels, and other necessities.

The larger the countertop, the more of an impact it makes. For smaller countertops, though, you may be able to use a more expensive material. Ceramic tile is a classic choice, but today you will also find glass tile, natural stone, fiber cement, metal, solid-surface, and plastic-laminate countertops. Wood can be used in a bathroom, but keep in mind that it will need to be sealed and may not fare as well if the room is subject to a lot of moisture, whether from steam or splashing.

Often-used countertops, like those on a vanity, should be strong and durable. Tile and flooring specialist Heather Loehr says, "Solid countertops, such as stone slabs, make for easy cleaning of surfaces in wet areas." She adds, "Decorative tiles can be more appropriately featured on backsplashes and shower walls and floors." These are good spots for unique designs, including those using three-dimensional tiles.

BATHTUBS AND SHOWERS These have evolved from utilitarian features to popular art features of the bathroom. If money or space is tight, it's possible to repair or refinish an existing tub. But if you're looking for something new, you will find styles and colors to match any decor. These include recessed or drop-in tubs, soaking tubs, and jetted tubs, as well as reproduction claw-foot tubs and walk-in tubs, ideal for those with disabilities.

A shower may be part of a tub or a separate feature. Many are large enough for more than one person. Even a smaller one can feature a bench. Steam showers are increasing in popularity, as

are dry saunas. If you have the room and dislike being closed in, consider an open shower. This type has no doors, simply a half wall or no wall. Curbless showers, where the floor extends into the shower area, are wheelchair accessible.

When choosing a showerhead, keep water conservation in mind. Low-flow showerheads are becoming more and more efficient. If more than one person will be showering at a time, add a second showerhead on a separate valve.

OPPOSITE PAGE, LEFT Reclaimed teak forms an organic counter and backsplash. Platinum-finish fixtures provide an elegant sheen.

OPPOSITE PAGE, RIGHT Marble countertops and a backsplash of glossy subway tiles amplify the natural light in this attic bath and help make the room feel larger than it is.

ABOVE LEFT A sleek skirt around the tub conceals the foam insulation that keeps the water hot.

ABOVE RIGHT A wide window opening to a small enclosed deck makes this shower feel like it's in its own private garden. The tawny slate tiles on the walls and floor accentuate the outdoor look and feel.

LEFT Natural stone and wood cabinetry lend an organic feel to this bathroom. A bamboo ladder towel rack carries the theme through the room.

TOP RIGHT Raised cabinetry and a framed mirror give a custom feel to this bathroom. Sconce lighting and artwork personalize the mostly neutral palette.

BOTTOM RIGHT Recycled-glass tiles in sage, green, gray, and chocolate frame the mirror; a solid-surface countertop and dark green cabinets underneath have complementary tones.

LEFT This narrow cantilevered trough sink was cast off-site and embedded with shells and rocks. The green tile is a soothing complementary shade.

RIGHT Tile, wainscoting, and paint combine to good effect in this master bath. The dark blue tile in the shower surround grounds the space and provides a nice contrast to the lighter walls in the rest of the room.

SINKS, FAUCETS, AND TOILETS These bathroom essentials can now be used to make a statement. Sinks come in a huge range of materials, from cast iron, porcelain enamel, and natural and engineered stone to steel, glass, concrete, metal, solid surface, and even wood. They can be set into a standard bathroom cabinet, retrofitted into a piece of furniture, even placed on top of the vanity. Pedestal sinks and wall-mounted sinks are good for small spaces. Because of the number of choices, it should be easy to find a sink style that fits with your personal style and decorating sensibility.

Faucets should match the sink style and bath fixtures. Polished chrome is the most popular choice, but you'll also find polished or burnished nickel, brass, and bronze fixtures. Look for quality fixtures, with solid brass workings and ceramic disks. Faucets should be equipped with a low-flow aerator that reduces the amount of water coming out, or you can add one. Look for aerators that have the WaterSense label and meet EPA guidelines.

While toilets seem to last forever, it may be time to replace yours. Newer models meet the federally mandated 1.6 gallons per flush, and, unlike earlier "low-flow" toilets, they're much more efficient and there are more options to choose from.

Two-piece toilets are the most common, but you can find one-piece designs, a good look in a contemporary room. Other options include elongated bowls and square profiles. Wall-hung toilets are also available, and give the room a minimalist look. White is still the most popular color choice.

Added Details

Once you've decided on the layout and main features of the bathroom, it's time to consider the remaining design details. Because they cover so much of the room, wall and floor covering choices will have the most impact. Choose colors that work well with the overall palette you've established, and look for materials that offer ease of maintenance. You'll also

want to think about both natural and artificial light sources.

WALLS AND FLOORS For walls, paint is the fastest and most durable way to go. A neutral tone will tie the other elements together, a bold color will make a statement. Semigloss and satin sheens are easiest to clean, but the higher the gloss, the more obvious the imperfections.

Walls can also be finished with tile, wood or wood look-alikes, and wallpaper.

Ceramic, porcelain, and glass tiles will all work well too, especially inside a bath or shower, and stone is increasingly popular. Glazed and glass tiles in particular are easy to clean, and a row of decorative tiles will add a special touch. Tile and flooring specialist Heather Loehr suggests, "Use a clear glass enclosure when specifying decorative tile in a tub/shower area. This way the shower walls can be seen and serve as artwork for the space."

Beadboard is a great choice for an older home or a cottage- or beach-inspired bathroom. Larger wood planks are also a good choice for a natural look. Both beadboard and planks will need to be painted or sealed. Wallpaper will give a vintage look but be sure to choose one that can handle moisture.

Flooring in a bathroom takes a lot of abuse. The top choices are ceramic, porcelain, and glass tiles. Look for tiles that are designed and rated for floor use, and

be sure they are slip-resistant. Stone floors are better for bathrooms that don't get much use; choose a matte, not a glossy, stone from a local quarry for eco-friendliness.

Other flooring choices include concrete, laminate, rubber tiles, linoleum, and vinyl. Wood can be used, but it's not a practical choice for most people. Green choices include terrazzo floors that mix concrete with recycled glass or porcelain, bamboo, and cork.

FAR LEFT A double-sided vanity mirror allows this homeowner to maintain her view. One side opens to reveal a medicine cabinet while the other side is the mirror.

LEFT Niches built to house towels match cabinetry artfully while providing a functional element.

BELOW Mixing vintage plumbing with contemporary sconce lighting creates a romantic, yet eclectic, vibe in this bathroom and vanity space.

LIGHTING You'll want general ambient light as well as task lighting for activities such as putting on makeup and shaving. The ideal is a mix of overhead lights and sconces. Choose styles that match the rest of your decor, especially for lights over the vanity, and consider adding dimmers.

Lighting specialist Zack Rosson says, "Layered light on dimmers creates the most versatility in a bathroom. Recessed cans with pendant or sconce lighting on a mirror can be controlled for shaving and applying makeup."

Natural light is always welcome in a bathroom, but you'll want to provide privacy as well. Glass blocks and frosted glass will eliminate the need for curtains. Shutters and blinds will allow some light in while blocking the view inside. If you go for a soft treatment, such as curtains or shades, choose a fabric that isn't transparent and can handle the inevitable moisture.

Finishing Touches

These include medicine cabinets, mirrors, hardware, and other accessories. Here's where small changes can have a large impact on the overall style of the room.

Medicine cabinets often sit behind the vanity mirror, providing extra storage in a convenient location. Consider dressing them up with trim or paint. Or, install an antique wall-hung cabinet that might have graced a hall or entryway.

Mirrors, too, can be simple and utilitarian or great style statements. If you have two sinks, adding an individual framed mirror over each will give your room a more updated and upscale image. To set your bathroom apart, consider a mirror with a specialty frame, whether it's made from branches to bring in a natural look or has colorful gems glued around the edge.

Hardware seems like a small detail, but it can make a big impression. Match the hardware style to the style of your room, using such materials as polished nickel in a beach-inspired bathroom, wood in a traditional bath, or sleek metal on a contemporary vanity. For a child's bath, add a touch of whimsy with bright colors or fun shapes.

The final details in a bathroom can be the most fun—and also can be the most easily changed. These include such things as towels and towel bars, shower curtains, bath mats and rugs, plus soap and toothbrush holders and bath and shower caddies. Take the time to find quality products that fit in well with your decor. You'll use the bathroom daily, so it's worth it to have the best touches you can afford.

Universal Design

It makes sense to incorporate universal design features into any bathroom remodel. These include nonslip flooring, handheld showerheads, and rocker switches, as well as easily operated knobs and levers and scald-free shower and tub valves. If you're opening walls around the shower, tub, and toilet area, add plywood reinforcement and bracing between wall studs so you can install grab bars, if needed. Wall-hung sinks, barrier-free showers, and shower seats are all stylish universal design options.

ABOVE LEFT Grab bars, a wall-hung sink, and an open shower are classic universal design elements.

ABOVE RIGHT A seat in the shower is useful to those with limited strength.

RIGHT Coils wrapped around the drainpipe under this sink protect the legs of someone in a wheelchair when the pipe gets hot.

BELOW A barrier-free shower has a clean and open aesthetic that is appealing.

Work Spaces

A home office can be carved out of the smallest of spaces. Here, office essentials are easily housed in the covered storage, on the floating shelf, and in the almost-hidden drawer built into the work surface.

TOP Bold color and pattern are inspiring to some. This brightly colored space reflects the character and interests of its inhabitant.

BOTTOM LEFT A bright stool is handy for working, and easy to move elsewhere when other seating is needed. The low profile and thin support legs keep the desk from overwhelming the corridor space.

BOTTOM RIGHT Built-in dividers make organization easy in this small office nook tucked into the corner of a kitchen.

The line between working in and living in our homes has become less distinct. More and more people want to have a home office, whether it's a simple space for taking care of household business, a spot for the inevitable papers and projects that make their way home from the workplace, or a dedicated spot for a full-time business.

A well-designed office can provide a space that encourages productivity and reflects the style of the rest of your home. Finding space, though, can be a challenge. If you're fortunate to have a spare room, it's easy to locate an office there.

All too often, you'll need to borrow space from an existing room—diplomatically, so as not to disturb the room's original purpose. A common spot is a corner of a kitchen or family room. The advantage is that the office is not separated from the day-to-day activities in the house; it also allows parents to monitor children's Internet usage. A corner of a guest bedroom is another popular choice. If your guest room must do double duty, look for furniture that keeps the room from being too businesslike, such as an office armoire, chests, cabinets, side tables, and footstools with built-in storage.

Space for home offices can also be found in some unexpected places, such as an underused closet, space under the stairs, or a place in the attic, basement, or garage.

Designing a Work Space

Some experts have said that there are only two essentials for a functional home office: a comfortable chair and a door that closes. Most people probably have a few more requirements. General contractor John Slaughter says, "Basic elements of designing a room include smart space planning, adequate lighting, and sufficient storage. When thinking of the home office, also consider functionality and inspirational comfort."

Start with your work surface. Stock desk units come in a variety of materials, but may be difficult to fit in with your room. Modular office furniture is more flexible and is available in a number of styles. Or look to repurpose furniture—flea-market finds and antiques can be turned, with some judicious changes, into acceptable home office elements.

Chairs need to be functional, but an office chair isn't your only choice. If you'll be spending a lot of time working in the office, choose an ergonomic chair with an adjustable seat and armrests to protect your spine and help reduce aches and injuries.

Make a list of everything you need, from pencils and paper clips to research materials and file folders. Measure all the electronic equipment you'll require to see where it will fit best. And make sure you allow for proper lighting. Natural light is great, but you'll need ambient and task lighting too. Watch out for the possibility of glare, especially when finding a place for your computer screen.

If the space doesn't have a door, you can establish a sense of privacy by the way you orient your work surface or by using a screen or file cabinets to mark off the area.

LEFT A salvaged desk and an eclectic mix of containers for pencils, papers, and other office necessities are low-cost choices for an eco-friendly office.

BOTTOM LEFT A beamed ceiling adds a sense of spaciousness to this home office; the long counter provides plenty of work space in a small room.

BOTTOM RIGHT A neat wall of storage holds projects, reference materials, and supplies. Bins contain miscellaneous objects that can easily get lost, and the shelves are both decorative and functional.

OPPOSITE PAGE, TOP When a home office space has a polished appearance, it's a joy to work in and inviting for clients. Projects and books are easily accessible here, but the room's overall feel is orderly and organized.

OPPOSITE PAGE, BOTTOM Though the furnishings in this home office work well with the flow of the home, pocket doors allow the room to be easily closed off when needed. Rustic, repurposed furnishings add charm to the space while remaining functional.

Play Spaces

If you have a hobby you enjoy, consider turning a room or a corner of a room into a dedicated space. For a yoga enthusiast, this room has space to work on poses and a relaxing seat for meditating when the session is done.

Play spaces include recreational spaces for both children and adults, hobby and craft rooms, workout rooms, and wine cellars. If you have the space, even if it's just an alcove, you can turn it into a well-used spot that will enrich your home.

You may have space for a traditional rec room, where both adults and children can gather. If so, divide the space into zones, with an area for more active play and an area for quieter activities. In the former, you might have a television and computer, a pool table, even a place to play musical instruments. The latter might consist of a couple of comfortable chairs and a reading lamp.

Add tables and chairs that can be used for drawing and painting, scrapbooking, or game night. Provide small children with low, washable tables for projects and create cubbies for handy toy storage. If you're going to be in the room often and it's far from the kitchen, consider installing a small refrigerator and a microwave for enjoying quick snacks. Make sure the seating is comfortable and plentiful and that the surface finishes can take hard wear and tear.

Hobby and craft rooms are becoming more and more popular. When designing the space, always plan for more storage than you'll need, whether it's for thread, fabric, and scissors; papers and photo supplies; or painting and sculpting materials. Keep the room organized with bins and baskets on shelves. Closets can also be transformed into storage with added shelving and wire baskets attached to the doors. This room can also be a place for a compact gift-wrap center, with paper, bows, and tags in easy reach and a solid surface for wrapping.

You will want to have an area to spread out your projects, but also a way to control the clutter when the room isn't in use. And don't forget to make sure the space is a fun place to work in.

ABOVE A swing inside the home creates a fun environment for kids and adults alike. In this room, even the wall and fabric colors are energetic.

RIGHT A chalkboard wall serves as a message center for all family members.

BELOW Cabinets, shelves, and deep drawers built into a laundry room offer ample storage for crayons, paints, and scrapbooking and sewing supplies.

INTERIOR DESIGNER
JENNIFER HILGARDNER ON

Craft Rooms

A craft room can be a functional space, but still have a whimsical, creative feel by the way it is designed. Fun paint colors and furniture can lead to creativity because the person will want to be in that space."

Utility Rooms

Utilitarian spaces, like laundry rooms and mudrooms, seldom receive the attention they deserve, which is odd when you consider how often they are used. A properly planned utility room can be a complete housekeeping area that simplifies your household chores.

These rooms may even serve multiple purposes. A mudroom may double as a grooming center for the family pets and a storage room for sports gear. An overhead rack in a laundry room can be used for drying flowers as well as clothes, and the sink can be turned into a potting center.

Mudrooms

A mudroom is the ideal storage space for shoes, lunch bags, sports equipment, and pet essentials such as food dishes, leashes, blankets, and toys. You don't even need an entire room to reap a mudroom's benefits. A narrow hall, a partial wall, even space carved out from between wall studs will do just fine.

Instead of letting a mudroom become cluttered, take advantage of its potential. Counters, tables, and benches can be storage pieces that collect and organize both day-to-day and seasonal items. A built-in cabinet that resembles a set of lockers will allow individual family members to have their own space. Other essentials for the room might include an umbrella stand, boot tray, baskets, and a chalk or message board.

Many cost-effective storage solutions are tailored specifically for utility spaces. You'll find a wealth of inexpensive storage ideas, such as wall-mounted racks for boots, shelving for hats, and hooks for sports gear, at home centers and container stores.

OPPOSITE PAGE A corner of a garage was turned into a wood-storage area, mudroom, and message center.

TOP RIGHT An effective mudroom provides a storage place for everything kid-related. Bins and baskets can house shoes, backpacks, and sports gear, while a chalkboard is handy for communicating with other family members.

BOTTOM RIGHT Personalized mudroom cubbies make it easy for everyone to know where their own jackets, hats, and boots should be as they come and go.

Laundry Rooms

A full-size laundry room offers more options than just doing laundry.

If there's space for more than appliances and a sink, add a table or table-height shelf for folding laundry, wrapping gifts, or potting plants. Add additional shelves or cabinets to store supplies. A drying rack over the sink that folds up against the wall makes it easy to hang clothing directly out of the washing machine. If there's room, add a rack for hanging clothes and even an ironing board.

You may spend a lot of time in this area, so make sure it's attractive. Interior designer Jennifer Hilgardner suggests painting it a vibrant color that draws you in or a soothing color that calms. Wall sayings or murals are a fun way to add interest. She also adds, "Laundry rooms are more functional if organized. Use clear jars for clothespins, sewing items, and detergent. Choose various heights to add interest."

A great, inexpensive design idea is to hang black-and-white photos with clothespins. Place the photos around the room as a border or on one wall for a gallery look.

Outdoor Rooms

The sleeping porch, a feature of many Craftsman houses, is updated with contemporary styling and weatherproof drapery and upholstery.

According to landscape designer Matt Lemos, "Outdoor areas are often the last to receive design attention, "but they shouldn't be. Plan space for your lifestyle by incorporating ample seating, table surfaces, cushions, play areas, eating spots, and sunning areas." By carrying your design style outdoors, you can turn a patio, deck, or even a balcony into another room of the house.

Many outdoor spaces have become quite elaborate, including seating areas, fireplaces and firepits, full-size kitchens, and dining areas. If you have a pool, you may want to add a cabana. Or you may want space for a basketball court, bocce ball, or croquet. Even if your space isn't that elaborate, you can still create a relaxing spot for lounging and entertaining.

ABOVE LEFT A simple covered patio and bold outdoor fabrics create an alfresco dining space for homeowners.

TOP RIGHT This L-shaped deck off a master suite is a tropical retreat, with painted gray decking that sets off the periwinkle walls and rattan furniture.

BOTTOM RIGHT A vivid abstract mural of ceramic tiles in energetic colors adds life to the outdoor kitchen and provides a scenic view from the indoor kitchen.

Your overall design should be able to accommodate your family's favorite activities, from relaxing to children's games and entertaining. At the same time, it's important that your outdoor space provide the same sense of privacy as interior rooms do. Landscape designer Lemos suggests using evergreen plants and trees; their year-round foliage helps encourage outdoor living during colder months.

An increasing number of options are available for furnishings designed to look like indoor furniture and fabrics while still being sturdy enough to handle outdoor conditions. You can also use indoor furniture, but, to protect it from bad weather, you may need to seal it, keep it under cover, or bring it indoors at times.

Even in a small space, delineate different areas for different activities. Build a patio with multiple levels—one for dining,

another for gathering around a firepit—or turn a side yard into a gravel-lined retreat. A table and chairs may sit near the barbecue while, on the other side of the space, lounge chairs, chaises, even a repurposed bed can offer a spot for relaxing, chatting with friends, or spending nights under the stars. An enclosed bench can provide hidden storage as well as seating, while a small water feature will add a sense of calmness and peace to the area. Plants can act as screens, as well as create a sense of depth along the perimeter.

Above all, an outdoor room should flow naturally from your home. Use colors and materials that blend well with your interior design. Keep the styles similar, choosing traditional Adirondack chairs for a cottage look or sleek and low lounges for a contemporary feel.

OPPOSITE PAGE, TOP LEFT A family room moves outdoors. The couch, chair, coffee tables, and rug would be equally at home indoors, but the materials are weather resistant.

OPPOSITE PAGE, TOP RIGHT A sunken dining area set into a deck is the centerpiece of this space. The table is a salvaged glass door atop ceramic planters; the seating is created from the deck itself. Overhead, bamboo fencing forms the roof of what the owners call their cabana.

OPPOSITE PAGE, BOTTOM LEFT A screened-in porch, furnished in the same style as the home's interior, adds square footage to the house and an open-air seating area.

OPPOSITE PAGE, BOTTOM RIGHT Large-scale furniture with clean lines creates a feeling of expansiveness in this small patio space. The result is modern, warm, and comfortable.

RIGHT A side-yard nook is a perfect dining spot. The tablecloth echoes the color of the cannas, fuchsias, and impatiens that surround it.

Move Your Indoors Out

A mix of tropical and tropical-like plants surround the space, adding color and fragrance to the patio.

OPPOSITE PAGE, TOP Rattan chairs add a light touch that balances the heavier lounging bed.

OPPOSITE PAGE, BOTTOM LEFT A pot found in Turkey that was converted to a fountain is mounted on a concrete pedestal in a 4-foot-square pool.

OPPOSITE PAGE, BOTTOM RIGHT The sleek portable grill doesn't overwhelm the space.

Interior designer Antonio Martins believes a garden should be personal. "It's more important for a garden to have meaning for you than for it to be in fashion," he says.

This philosophy is reflected in his small 25- by 25-foot backyard. Everything in the space has a history, whether it's a table made from a redwood round he found, plants he found at arboretum

sales, or the garden mascot, his neighbor's Congo African Grey parrot. Martins, who grew up in Brazil surrounded by tropical forests, and who has also lived in Asia, combined these finds with

elements from both cultures to create a space for dining, conversing, and relaxing with a good book. The result resembles a verdant corner of a luxe resort.

The Elements

- **Seating:** A teak daybed from Bali anchors the seating area; all-weather rattan chairs give the garden a breezy resort look.

- **Tables:** The tables are made from recycled materials. The coffee table was fashioned from recycled teak railroad ties; a redwood side table is mounted on a salvaged rusted-steel pedestal.

- **Flooring:** Seven different sizes of travertine pavers are arranged in a random pattern.

- **Lighting:** Lanterns and candles illuminate the space.

- **Accessories:** A mirror set into a wood frame carved in Brazil sits over the lounge and creates the illusion of space. A pot fountain from Turkey adds a water element, and a portable grill doubles as a heat source at night.

Surfaces

Floors and walls are the largest surfaces in your home. How you treat them, whether as a backdrop for furnishings or as a strong statement that takes center stage, will have an impact on all other features in a room. Although window treatments do not cover as large an area, they will also be a prominent feature of the room's overall look and feel. Taking the time to learn about different wall and floor finishes will allow you to make choices that enhance your home's design.

Beautiful floor coverings can truly transform a room. They can also be one of your biggest expenses, so planning ahead is essential. Before deciding on materials, colors, and textures, consider some design basics.

Using a single type of flooring throughout most of your home, breaking it only at bedrooms and wet areas, will create the biggest impact. Solid colors make a room seem more spacious, and a solid color is easier to decorate around. Light colors exude spaciousness and help brighten a room, while dark colors help anchor furniture and make larger rooms feel cozier. If you choose to change the color or type of flooring between rooms, picture how the transition will look when the doors are open.

How a room is used will also affect your choice of finishes. For a kitchen, you want a floor that is easy to clean and resistant to water and other spills. Bathroom flooring needs to stand up to moisture. Flooring in family rooms, hallways, and children's bedrooms must be able to take more wear and tear than a living or dining room. And any room that opens directly to the outdoors needs flooring that can handle both dirt and heavy traffic.

Ceramic, stone, wood, and concrete floors are beautiful and long-wearing choices. Tile specialist Tracy Bowman notes, "Stone brings nature into your environment and wears well for generations." Resilient floors such as vinyl or linoleum or soft floors such as carpet are best in work areas, because they are more comfortable and warmer to stand on. Materials such as cork, rubber, vinyl, and cushion-back vinyl have good sound absorbency.

Ceramic and Stone Tile

For versatility and durability, there's nothing better than tile. It can be used in any room and with any design. It comes in a wide range of colors, textures, finishes, and prices. As Tracy Bowman notes, "Tile is universally appealing, sustainable, and easy to maintain."

Any tile rated for floor use will meet basic requirements for strength and slip resistance, but different materials have different pros and cons. Glazed ceramic tiles are impervious and wear-resistant; unglazed ceramic tiles are softer and must be sealed. Porcelain tiles are the most durable and maintenance-free choice. Glass tiles are generally used on walls, but there are some that can be used on floors.

OPPOSITE PAGE Natural hardwood planks warm up what could have been a stark space. Wood is a popular choice throughout a home, especially for people with allergies.

ABOVE Ceramic tiles are a practical choice for a bathroom.

RIGHT Large ceramic tiles look like stone at a fraction of the cost.

BELOW Porcelain tiles set in an alternating color pattern are a classic entry choice. The flat finish and smaller size make them more slip-resistant than other choices.

Natural stone tile includes limestone, slate, soapstone, marble, and granite. Glazed stone tiles are as durable as glazed ceramic tiles; others require sealing. Stone is also subject to weathering and aging, which many people prefer. As tile and flooring specialist Heather Loehr says, "Over time, natural stone develops a patina that is unique to the traffic patterns of the space. Just as for linen fabric and wood cabinetry, the natural look and wear only add to the product's beauty."

Tile is a hard surface, so fragile items are more likely to break when dropped on it. It can be cold to bare feet and noisy if no sound-absorbing underlayments are installed.

Wood

Beautiful but tough, wood is a warmer and more forgiving material than tile. There are two kinds of wood floors: solid wood and engineered wood. Both are eco-friendly options when certified by the FSC (Forest Stewardship Council). You can also choose floors salvaged from older buildings or milled from salvaged posts and beams.

Both solid- and engineered-wood floors come in different widths and finishes. The direction in which you lay the boards will automatically appear to lengthen or widen an area. When in doubt, create a dramatic effect and put it on the diagonal. Varying the direction of the wood grain throughout a room is not a good idea except to define specific areas.

Wood floors can be noisy and may be damaged by pets and hard use. Solid-wood floors can be refinished; options for refinishing engineered-wood floors are limited. To avoid polyurethane fumes, look for prefinished wood flooring.

Laminate

Laminate flooring is a photograph of another surface that is adhered to a base and then sealed. Inexpensive, resilient, and easy to install, laminate is popular with do-it-yourselfers. The higher-end products are more resistant to damage and will last longer. Adding an underlayment will absorb sound and make the flooring sound less hollow when walked on. Unlike wood, laminate cannot be refinished.

Linoleum and Vinyl

Linoleum is a classic flooring material that is making a comeback. It's ideal for renovations of older homes. The new linoleum is durable, as easy to maintain as vinyl, and available in a wide range of colors. Linoleum is a natural product, and its manufacturing and disposal involve no environmental toxins.

Because of the range of colors, low cost, and easy maintenance, vinyl has long been popular. However, the potential environmental hazards leave the product up for debate.

Wide wood planks set vertically along this hallway subtly reinforce the path to the door.

TILE AND FLOORING SPECIALIST
HEATHER LOEHR ON

Choosing Tiles

Larger-format tiles create a sense of spaciousness. Put the tile on a diagonal and the room will appear even larger and more welcoming. If you choose this layout, you will need to purchase 10 percent more tile due to the required perimeter cuts. Purchasing additional tiles is always a good idea anyway. You'll then have tiles to match if you need to make a repair."

ABOVE Wood flooring works well in a contemporary kitchen, providing a sleek appearance that coordinates with the cabinets, chairs, and countertops while adding a warm glow.

LEFT With its wide range of colors and patterns, sheet vinyl is a great choice for adding interest to a laundry room.

RIGHT Slate is a durable, hardworking tile; the glass-inset tile used here adds interest.

LEFT Concrete flooring can be tinted any color of the rainbow.

OPPOSITE PAGE, TOP Cork flooring is a good choice for a kitchen. It's naturally soft, which gives it a cushiony feel when you stand and walk on it. Here, it also ties in with the natural tones of the cabinetry.

OPPOSITE PAGE, MIDDLE An area rug of subtle color anchors and defines a sitting area.

OPPOSITE PAGE, BOTTOM Carpet tiles laid in a non-symmetrical pattern add dimension to a seating area.

Bamboo and Cork

Two of the most popular flooring choices today also happen to be the most environmentally friendly. Bamboo is made from certain varieties of Asian timber bamboo, a fast-growing grass. Planks are available in various lengths and widths. Bamboo is more durable than many hardwoods, although it, like wood, will expand and contract as moisture conditions change. Although it originally was manufactured in only blond tones, a number of vivid stains are now available. If you install bamboo in a kitchen or bath, seal the floor after installation, even if you buy finished planks.

Cork flooring is made from leftovers from the manufacturing of cork stoppers. The raw material comes from the bark of the cork oak tree, which can be harvested without harming the tree. The most eco-friendly cork tiles or planks use water-based pigments, varnishes, and adhesives. Cork is soft, sound absorbent, and warm to walk on; it is a natural insect repellent, and comes in a range of hues, from a soft honey to bright shades. It is also easy to install. Cork can be damaged if flooded, but will take occasional water. Look for prefinished and preglued varieties. Cork should be sealed after installation, even if it is presealed, and resealed yearly.

Concrete

Concrete is one of the most popular flooring choices today. It is extremely durable, and poured concrete can be tinted, stained, or etched to mimic stone or tile. It can also have pieces of stone, wood, or glass mixed in or embedded into it for a one-of-a-kind look. It is an extremely hard surface, so it will be noisy; any fragile items dropped on it will probably break. Consider pairing concrete with a radiant heating surface. You will also need to seal it regularly.

Rubber

Rubber flooring is available in tile and sheet forms and in a limited variety of color and textures. It is comparable to the cost of good-quality vinyl, and works well in kitchens, mudrooms, and home gyms because it is highly durable and both water- and slip-resistant. Look for tiles that contain no PVC (polyvinyl chloride) or virgin EPDM rubber.

Carpet and Area Rugs

A carpet provides the most warmth and comfort of any floor covering, and doesn't show dust like hard surfaces. Today's technologies have created an even greater variety of textures, colors, and cuts. Carpets made of woven plants and grasses, such as sisal, are now much more versatile. Stain-resistant finishes mean easy care and less worry.

Solid colors are always a safe choice, though they won't stand out. Patterned carpet will have an immediate impact when you enter a room. If the pattern is too busy, though, it will be difficult to decorate around. That being said, a beautiful carpet can be the focal point of any room.

A typical area rug is designed to cover large portions of the floor while still allowing part of it to show. Such rugs make a room feel cozy, especially over concrete, tile, or stone floors. Area rugs can be the centerpiece of a room, used to define one specific area within a room, or placed over an existing carpet to create added dimension. Interior designer Jennifer Hilgardner believes that "a well-chosen floor rug placed in the right spot can enhance anything you can dream up."

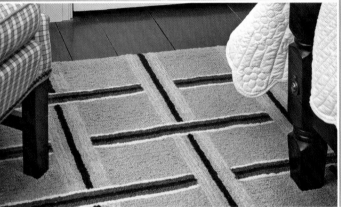

TOP LEFT A pale gray concrete floor catches the sunlight and opens up the room.

BOTTOM LEFT This area rug unifies the bedroom palette while providing a pattern that is complementary to all the fabrics.

ABOVE Bamboo flooring gives an organic serenity to this bedroom.

TOP RIGHT Gray rubber textured flooring covers the stairs; the same tiles, in bright yellow, line the wall.

BOTTOM RIGHT A plush dark blue rug contrasts perfectly with the warm wood floors.

Flooring at a glance

Ceramic Tile

- **Pros:** Broad range of sizes, shapes, and colors; durable; water-resistant
- **Cons:** Must choose styles with enough strength for floors; can be slippery; cold underfoot; grout is high maintenance
- **Price:** $–$$
- **Green Issues:** Look for tiles made of recycled materials or for salvaged or surplus tiles that would otherwise go to waste

Porcelain Tile

- **Pros:** Can mimic the look of stone; strong; water-resistant
- **Cons:** Cold underfoot; grout is high maintenance
- **Price:** $–$$
- **Green Issues:** More eco-friendly than natural stone

Glass Tile

- **Pros:** Stylish; unique; beautiful color palette
- **Cons:** Must choose styles with enough strength and slip resistance for floors; grout is high maintenance
- **Price:** $$–$$$
- **Green Issues:** Look for tiles made of recycled glass

Stone

- **Pros:** Luxurious; range of colors and patterns
- **Cons:** Color and veining can vary from what you see in the showroom; heavy; cold underfoot; must be resealed regularly
- **Price:** $$–$$$
- **Green Issues:** Most varieties are imported from overseas; choose one that's quarried close to home

Wood

- **Pros:** Wide variety of colors, grains, and plank widths; soft and warm underfoot; can be sanded and refinished several times
- **Cons:** Must be resealed regularly; can be damaged by hard use
- **Price:** $$–$$$
- **Green Issues:** Use water-based, low-VOC stains and finishes; buy FSC-certified or reclaimed wood flooring

Laminate

- **Pros:** Looks similar to hardwood, ceramic, or stone but can be less expensive; easy to maintain; somewhat stain-resistant
- **Cons:** Can't be refinished
- **Price:** $–$$
- **Green Issues:** Look for manufacturers who have FSC-certified or recycled-content fiberboard cores; avoid those that contain formaldehyde adhesives that offgas

Linoleum

- **Pros:** Wide variety of colors; made of natural materials; durable; biodegradable; warm and soft underfoot
- **Cons:** Linseed oil in linoleum gives off a slight odor that some find objectionable; must be resealed regularly
- **Price:** $–$$
- **Green Issues:** Linoleum is a wholly green material, from cradle to grave, although it is currently manufactured only in Europe, which means transportation emission issues are involved

Vinyl

- **Pros:** Warm and soft underfoot; doesn't need to be resealed
- **Cons:** Damaged tiles need to be replaced
- **Price:** $
- **Green Issues:** Made of PVC (polyvinyl chloride), which has serious environmental and health issues

Bamboo

- **Pros:** Looks similar to hardwood but is less expensive; can be sanded and refinished several times
- **Cons:** Limited color choices; must be resealed regularly to avoid water damage
- **Price:** $–$$
- **Green Issues:** Imported from Asia (carbon emission issues); some varieties contain formaldehyde adhesives that offgas

Cork

- **Pros:** Warm and soft underfoot; resists denting; has insulating qualities
- **Cons:** Must be resealed regularly
- **Price:** $–$$
- **Green Issues:** Uses a renewable and reconsidered waste material; choose manufacturers that don't use formaldehyde adhesives and do use no-VOC finishes

Concrete

- **Pros:** Can be stamped, textured, and colored; easy to clean

Slate is ideal for this mudroom—it's easy to clean yet durable enough to handle muddy boots and dripping umbrellas.

- **Cons:** Cold and hard underfoot (but can be warmed up with a radiant-heat system); must be resealed regularly
- **Price:** $$–$$$
- **Green Issues:** Ask your contractor to substitute recycled fly ash for some of the Portland cement to reduce CO_2 emissions by keeping fly ash out of landfills

Rubber

- **Pros:** Durable; water- and slip-resistant
- **Cons:** Certain types made from recycled tires have an odor; some styles are more suited to commercial and outdoor installations

- **Price:** $–$$
- **Green Issues:** Choose a type made with recycled and renewable materials that do not offgas

Carpet and Area Rugs

- **Pros:** Wide variety of colors and textures; soft and warm underfoot
- **Cons:** Harder to keep clean; carpet not recommended for moist areas
- **Price:** $–$$
- **Green Issues:** Choose carpets and rugs made of natural materials like wool or that contain recycled material

Walls

"A house is a home when it shelters the body and comforts the soul" - Phillip Moffitt

The wall treatment you choose can enhance your design choices in a way that no other single element can. Before you begin, think about the basics of the room: the quality of the light, the room's proportions, any architectural features you want to emphasize or downplay, and the furniture and fabrics you plan to use.

Color, texture, and trim all play a role in how your wall treatment works. Consider how you can use a range of surfaces and hues to enhance every room throughout your home. "Using a variety of surfaces and hues will create depth and interest in your home. In my entry, I have American Clay plaster; in the adjacent living room, I have the same color in a flat paint. It is the subtle texture difference that adds interest," says paint specialist Virginia Young. Finally, before deciding on any wall treatment, factor in how it will look and work in conjunction with how the room is used.

Wall Finishes

It used to be that the only fix for imperfect walls was wallpaper or wall repair. Imperfections, voids, dents, and dings can ruin a good paint job and used to take a long time to repair. There have been a whole host of improvements in the world of walls. Texturing is the new take on the old art of plastering. It's gotten easier and less expensive, so do-it-yourselfers now have lots of options to choose from.

SMOOTH Smooth wall finishes are the most labor-intensive and expensive, but also the most beautiful. There are two types of flat wall finishes: one for a standard paint treatment, which leaves a slight pebble finish; and one that is smoother, for wallpaper and many custom faux paint finishes, such as metallic, candlelit, and suede. A smooth finish is best for kitchens and bathrooms.

LEFT Contrasting paint colors and wall words personalize this bedroom.

TOP LEFT Plaster adds a variegated texture and patina to the walls of this home wine bar.

TOP RIGHT This angled wing wall is covered in a water-resistant pigmented plaster with a smooth-troweled finish.

BOTTOM Pigmented plaster lends a layered richness to surfaces, giving the colors a special radiance and depth. The technique can be used throughout a room (near right) or on only one wall as an accent (far right).

SKIP TROWEL Skip-trowel texture offers a more refined look under paint, and it's meant to add dimension to the finished look of the walls. This treatment is the most forgiving of drywall imperfections. A variety of textures can be created with any number of things: paint rollers, trowels with different notches, whisk brooms, ropes, and sea sponges.

ORANGE PEEL Orange peel is the term generally used to describe a "generic" texture that's good for hiding simple defects. Orange peel is a good choice for any paint job. Splatter drag is a rougher, less-detailed variation of orange peel, with many peaks and valleys that help add contrast to the paint finish.

LIGHT TO HEAVY TEXTURE Textured drywall ranges from light to heavy. Like plaster, textured finishes hide wall imperfections. Finish a textured surface with paint.

TRADITIONAL PLASTER On existing plaster walls, a fresh coat of plaster has always been the way to smooth out a bumpy or damaged finish. Traditional three-coat plaster jobs consist of a scratch coat, a brown coat, and a finish coat. The finish can be smooth or textured. Plasters may also be tinted before they are applied.

VENETIAN PLASTER Three or four razor-thin layers of plaster form a beautifully polished finish with an impressive richness and deepness that is often described as "burnished."

Paint

Traditional flat finishes add style to a room in a relatively easy manner. "We love how flat finishes absorb light, which accentuates the beauty and drama of deep, rich color," say paint specialists Virginia Young and Janie Lowe. But an expanse of solid color may not be what you are looking for. Decorative effects with subtle color variations can add depth and life to a room.

Decorative painting techniques are numerous and varied. Color washing uses layers of paint to achieve a rich patina. Sponging, ragging, and combing use household objects to apply or manipulate wet paints; dragging and stippling utilize dry brushes to achieve the effect. By stenciling and stamping, you can add graphic patterns to wall. Faux finishes mimic the look of other materials, such as wood or granite. Trompe l'oeil is painting an object or scene so realistically that it "tricks the eye," making viewers believe that what they see is real.

Wallpaper

Wallpaper is wonderfully versatile. It comes in a wide assortment of patterns, from stripes and florals to abstracts and murals. It is a good choice for a traditional room, but new designs, including grass papers, textured vinyls, flocked finishes, and embossed designs, can also work well in a contemporary space. Wallpaper also hides wall imperfections.

Eco-Friendly Paints

VOCs (volatile organic compounds) are the solvents in most paints that evaporate and contribute to the depletion of the ozone. VOCs also cause an unpleasant paint odor, and they continue to offgas and contribute to poor indoor air quality. "Walls are approximately 70 percent of a home's interior surface. Using low- or no-VOC paint is key to better indoor air quality. Today we build our homes so efficiently that we trap the VOCs from paints, as well as those from carpet and cabinetry, in our homes, leading to indoor air pollution," says Janie Lowe of Yolo Colorhouse, a maker of nature-inspired, eco-friendly paints.

RIGHT An old shed became a colorful test canvas for a line of eco-friendly exterior paint hues.

ABOVE Bright wall color adds a cheery touch to a simple powder room.

OPPOSITE PAGE, LEFT Board-and-batten walls on the interior give a rustic yet clean beach feel to this pool house.

OPPOSITE PAGE, TOP RIGHT A monochromatic leaf pattern in this wall covering is an elegant and organic backdrop in a bathroom.

OPPOSITE PAGE, BOTTOM RIGHT Higher-than-usual beadboard wainscoting topped by paint is a classic look for a traditional bathroom.

When choosing a wallpaper, think about the colors you want in the room, the textures you have in fabrics and other furnishings, and the amount of wall space to be covered. Put a sample on the wall and live with it in different light conditions and with the other materials you will be using in the room before committing, especially if the pattern is prominent.

Keep in mind that, once installed, wallpaper is more difficult to change than paint. Patterned wallpaper may also become dated. If you choose a pattern, such as subtle stripes, grasscloth, or small shapes, be sure it won't conflict with displayed art and photographs.

Other Options

Paint and wallpaper aren't your only wall-covering options. Explore the possibility of using stone or ceramic tile, commonly used in bathrooms, in other rooms in the house. Look at incorporating wood or metal, either on its own or as an accent in combination with a more traditional wall covering. For something unique, upholster a wall in panels. This makes a great headboard in a bedroom and is unexpected in an office or a family room. Creative hide specialist Kyle Bunting recommends hides for walls: "It's warm and luxurious."

LEFT White painted wood-trim pieces can be combined to create a gallery effect. The combination of the chair railing, casing, and crown molding completes the look of this stairway.

OPPOSITE PAGE, TOP Baseboards fill the gap between wood flooring and the softly colored walls in this bedroom.

OPPOSITE PAGE, BOTTOM LEFT This bathroom's wainscoting ties into the cabinetry on both sides of the room and creates a backdrop to the claw-foot tub.

OPPOSITE PAGE, BOTTOM RIGHT A wide chair railing coupled with wainscoting can work double duty as an art shelf. Frame the top with crown molding as shown in this hallway.

Trims and Woodwork

The first rule in choosing trim and wood-work is to match the style of your home. You may love deep crown molding and a center medallion on the ceiling, but this probably would not work in a contemporary or ranch-style home. A modern home should have plain moldings with little detail. Traditional homes look wonderful with deep baseboards and wide casings. Elegant period-style homes are enhanced with very detailed decorative moldings.

BASEBOARD True to its name, baseboard molding is installed at the bottom of a wall against the flooring to cover the gap between the two surfaces. Baseboards also protect against wall wear and tear when floors are cleaned. They range from 2 to 6 inches deep.

CASING Casing fills the gap between a window and a wall or a door and a wall. Typically, casings are between 1 and 4 inches wide. Cased openings provide a nice contrast to whatever wall color you choose.

CROWN MOLDING This is used to fill the gap between a wall and the ceiling. Crown moldings can measure from 1½ inches deep to up to 15 or 20 inches deep; they should be chosen based on the size of the room, the height of the ceiling, and the overall grandness of the space. A typical home uses crown moldings that are 4 to 5 inches deep.

CHAIR RAILING Chair railings run parallel to the floor, approximately 30 to 36 inches up from the floor. Their original purpose was to protect the wall from chairs bumping against it. Today, they are used for decorative purposes, and are most effective when there is a difference between the upper and lower sections of the wall. This difference can

be created with paint color, either different hues of the same color or different colors; with wallpaper; or with a combination of paint and wallpaper.

WAINSCOTING This old-style wood paneling runs from the floor partially up the wall. The usual height is 36 or

48 inches, but some historic installations are 6 to 8 feet high. Wainscoting can be formed from individual tongue-and-groove boards or raised panels. It is trimmed out at the foot with baseboard and at the top with chair railing or cap molding.

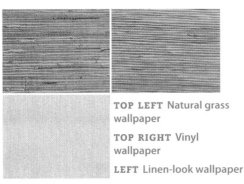

LEFT Wide pine boards are the perfect rustic touch in a cabin bedroom.

ABOVE White painted beams echo the white trim used throughout this kitchen and help elongate the space visually.

RIGHT Rough concrete shaped to resemble boards provides a foil for the smooth steel edging that sits next to it.

Wall Finishes at a glance

Paint

- **Pros:** Quick and inexpensive
- **Cons:** Won't cover up damage on a wall
- **Price:** $
- **Green Issues:** Buy low- or no-VOC paint to avoid problems with indoor air quality

Wallpaper

- **Pros:** A quick way to add color and texture to walls; works well in period homes
- **Cons:** If moisture gets behind wallpaper, a mold problem can develop
- **Price:** $–$$$
- **Green Issues:** Vinyl wallpaper is made of PVC, which has serious environmental and health issues; use nonvinyl wallpaper in powder rooms and half baths

Wainscoting

- **Pros:** Can be created with wood or tile
- **Cons:** If wood, must be kept sealed in bathrooms to avoid moisture damage
- **Price:** $–$$
- **Green Issues:** Buy MDF (medium-density fiberboard) panels that do not contain formaldehyde, or use reclaimed or FSC-certified wood; finish with a low- or no-VOC paint or stain

TOP LEFT Natural grass wallpaper

TOP RIGHT Vinyl wallpaper

LEFT Linen-look wallpaper

Tile

- **Pros:** Ceramic tile comes in a broad range of sizes, shapes, and colors; porcelain tile can mimic the look of stone; stone is luxurious; all are durable
- **Cons:** Grout is high maintenance; color and veining on stone can vary from what you see in the showroom
- **Price:** $–$$$
- **Green Issues:** Look for tiles made of recycled materials or for salvaged or surplus tiles that would otherwise go to waste; most stone is imported from overseas, contributing to carbon emission issues, so choose stone that's quarried close to home

TOP LEFT Pale blue grasscloth softens the entry hall in a contemporary home.

TOP RIGHT Crown molding on a drop soffit above the fireplace lends a sense of stateliness. Semi-gloss paint adds a formal feel to the entire room.

LEFT Thin chair railing is sometimes used as a decorative element below crown molding, as seen just above the window in this bedroom.

Window Treatments

Windows not only let light and air into our homes, they expand the sense of interior spaciousness while framing our view of the world beyond. But for all their benefits, windows present a few aesthetic and practical challenges. Uncovered, they admit harsh sunlight, passing glances, and chilling drafts. Bare windows can appear cold and unfinished. For both beauty and function, most need window treatments.

Whether airy and open or dramatically draped, window treatments help define the style and mood of a room. Your options are many. When deciding on a window treatment, start with an overview of style possibilities, then think about color and design. Don't forget hardware choices as well—they can add just the right finishing touch.

Whether you go for graceful swags, simple panels, hard-working blinds, or traditional curtains, your window

LEFT Unexpected sheer draperies capture light and create a shimmery effect in a room.

TOP RIGHT A simple stagecoach valance can provide both color and texture. Using a fabric that's darker than the surrounding wall color turns the window into a special accent.

BOTTOM RIGHT Windows over the bed, which open into the room in an unusual twist, are high enough to not need window treatments. The larger windows on either side are fitted with simple wood blinds to match the overall rustic feel of the room.

treatments must be appropriate to the room—not overdone in a room that's short on architectural details, and not skimpy in a room on a grand scale. Rooms with high ceilings offer more options. Fortunately, there are lovely window treatments for small-scale rooms too, and using beautiful materials and insisting on careful workmanship will elevate even the simplest design.

The first step in choosing a window treatment is to decide how much privacy and light control you need. For a room in which minimal privacy is needed, maximize the available natural light and select sheer fabrics that let the sun stream in. For more privacy and a cozy effect, create a soft wall of opaque texture and rich color. For a richer effect, choose a double drapery rod, which allows you to layer a sheer drape under a heavier one for added depth and maximum light control. But be sure to let your windows breathe. If you overdress them with yards of fabric, they will quickly feel heavy and seem dated.

Curtains

Both curtains and drapes consist of panels of fabric; it is how they are attached at the top that determines which category they fall into. Curtains are gathered on a rod or attached to it by tabs, ties, or rings. They are generally stationary; if they are opened and closed, it is done by hand.

Curtains can be as simple as a flat panel tied back above the sash, be pleated to resemble a drape, or be voluminous creations. They can also be any length, from cafe style, which covers only the lower half of a window, to panels that end at the sash, to full-length curtains that reach the floor. Curtains combine well with other treatments, such as blinds and shades. Cornices and valances add a finished touch.

Drapes

These are the mainstay of window fashions. By definition, drapes are pleated panels that hang from hooks that attach to small slides on a rod. You open and close the panels by a cord that moves the slides along a track. The rod itself may either be covered by the panel or exposed. Pinch-pleated styles are traditional, but numerous variations exist.

When it comes to choosing a drape, a layered look delivers the most options. Besides allowing excellent light control, layering is a creative way to bring color and contrast to windows. Pair a light-colored inner sheer with a rich outer layer of velvet or silk, or match hues to create a tone-on-tone effect.

The length of your drapes can have great impact. For a clean, casual look, hang drapes so they just touch the floor. For a more dramatic effect, allow the fabric to puddle 4 to 6 inches on the floor in luxurious folds.

With the variety of rods available these days, it is easy to find the right hardware to finish off the window. The size of the room, the height of the windows, and the scale of the treatment will suggest the appropriate rods and rings. You can mount rods directly to the window frame or to the wall above it, depending on the look you want to achieve. To create the illusion of added height, interior designer Jennifer Hilgardner suggests that you hang the rod slightly higher than the window frame.

It is more pleasing to the eye to place tiebacks on draperies above the center (about one-third of the way down) or below the center (about two-thirds of the way down). It's prettier to have a long fall of fabric going into or coming out of the tieback rather than cutting the fall of fabric precisely in half.

LEFT Soft sheers are a traditional touch in a contemporary room.

RIGHT Crisp white cafe curtains fit the early 20th-century style of this remodeled kitchen.

BELOW LEFT Curtain panels can be easily installed on rings with clips. Line panels to help them hang more smoothly and to decrease the amount of light that comes through when they are closed.

BELOW RIGHT Drapes and a valance over the bed add grandeur to a small bedroom.

LEFT Wood blinds add a natural and organic touch to this cozy nook. The simple design doesn't detract from the patterns in the rest of the room.

BELOW A one-of-a-kind stencil design brightens up a plain roller shade. Adding your own design will make your shades unique.

Shades

Shades are one of the most practical and hardworking window treatments. They offer easy light control, instant privacy, and a clean, tailored silhouette in a wide range of colors and fabrics. Options are versatile and varied, and include simple roller shades, insulated honeycomb shades, woven shades, wooden shades, and soft fabric shades, including Roman, balloon, and cloud shades.

Shades are a good choice if windows don't allow a fuller treatment, such as corner windows without much space between them. They're also a good choice for a clean, uncluttered look, or when you want to use a fabric with a large pattern or motif, because they will help show off the fabric. Naturally woven blinds and shades have a handmade feel and an organic texture. They also provide rooms with filtered light because of their uneven structure.

Be sure your shades are constructed with childproof cords, hidden side hems, and durable linings. They can be mounted inside the window frame or on the wall or molding outside the frame. The general rule, according to Jennifer Hilgardner, is to add 2 to 3 inches to the overall width of the shade to allow room for mounting hardware.

Blinds and Shutters

Blinds and shutters have adjustable louvers and vanes that can be tilted to filter the light, leveled to reveal the view, or shifted to completely block the view. Blinds can be used on their own or under top treatments made of fabric. Horizontal blinds made of vinyl or metal come in a wide array of finishes and colors; vertical blinds also come in an array of textures and materials and create a contemporary look. Wood blinds mimic the look of shutters but at a lower cost.

Shutters add architectural interest and drama to a window. They're available in wood and vinyl. Traditional shutters with 1½-inch louvers provide privacy but cut down on light and the view. Plantation shutters have wider louvers, 2½- and 3½-inch sizes, which allow better ventilation and a clearer view.

Valances and Cornices

These top treatments provide the crowning glory for a window. Valances are generally shortened versions of curtains, drapes, or fabric shades, 12 to 18 inches long at the center and may be longer at the sides. Used alone, they bring style to an otherwise plain window. Placed over another treatment, they conceal the heading and add a flourish. Tab-top, tie-top, or rod-pocket styles are popular in casual settings, while inverted box pleats that are board mounted provide a tailored look. Swags also fall into this category, but can make a window feel heavy and dated.

Because their edges are so clearly delineated, cornices add architectural interest. Like valances, they can be used alone or paired with other window treatments. When covered in batting and fabric, cornices soften the overall look of the window. Depending on your fabric choice and whether you choose a straight or scalloped edge, they can give a casual, tailored, or formal look to a window. Wood cornices mimic the look of deep crown molding and should coordinate with the other woodwork and trim in the room.

Hardware

All types of window treatments need hardware. This can be as simple as a spring-loaded rod, ideal for a cafe curtain, or as elaborate as a top rod that outshines the window treatment itself. Hardware that will be covered by fabric is generally plain and unobtrusive. Other hardware is more decorative, including styles with elaborate finials. When choosing the latter, look for hardware that blends well with your windows and the rest of the room's decor.

Measuring Windows

To estimate the amount of fabric you need or to order window treatments, you need to measure your windows. The best approach is to work directly from the window measurement rather than from the hardware. You will get the most accurate results by using a retractable steel tape measure.

For a treatment mounted inside the window, measure the width of the opening (A) and the length (B).

If your treatment will hang outside the window opening, as most do, measure the area to be covered to the left (C) and right (D) of the opening and the distance above the opening (E). The top of the treatment is usually even with the top of the trim board, but you may also mount a treatment just below the ceiling, at the bottom of the crown molding, or halfway between the ceiling and the window opening.

The distance below the opening (F) varies, depending on the treatment style. Some treatments end at the windowsill. Apron-length treatments usually end 4 inches below the opening. Floor-length treatments usually end ¼ to 1 inch from the floor, but if you want the panels to puddle on the floor, allow several extra inches when measuring.

If you want a fuller curtain, purchase panels double the width of your windows. Fuller panels always provide more drama. The higher the ceiling, the fuller the drape body should be—it is all a matter of proportion.

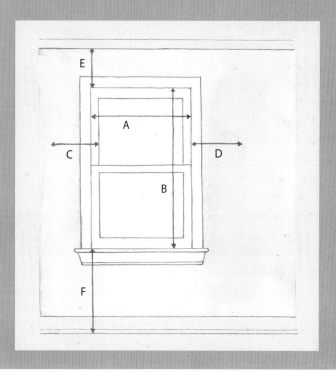

Chapter 4

Palettes

Nothing changes a room more than color. Color can be bold and dramatic, like a classic red, or subtle, like a soft mocha. Warm colors wrap a room like a blanket while cool colors create a sense of calm. How you use color depends on your personal preferences. You don't need much color to make a significant color statement. If your favorite color is too strong for an entire room, use it as an accent by painting the inside of a cupboard or the outside of a picture frame or mirror.

Choosing Colors

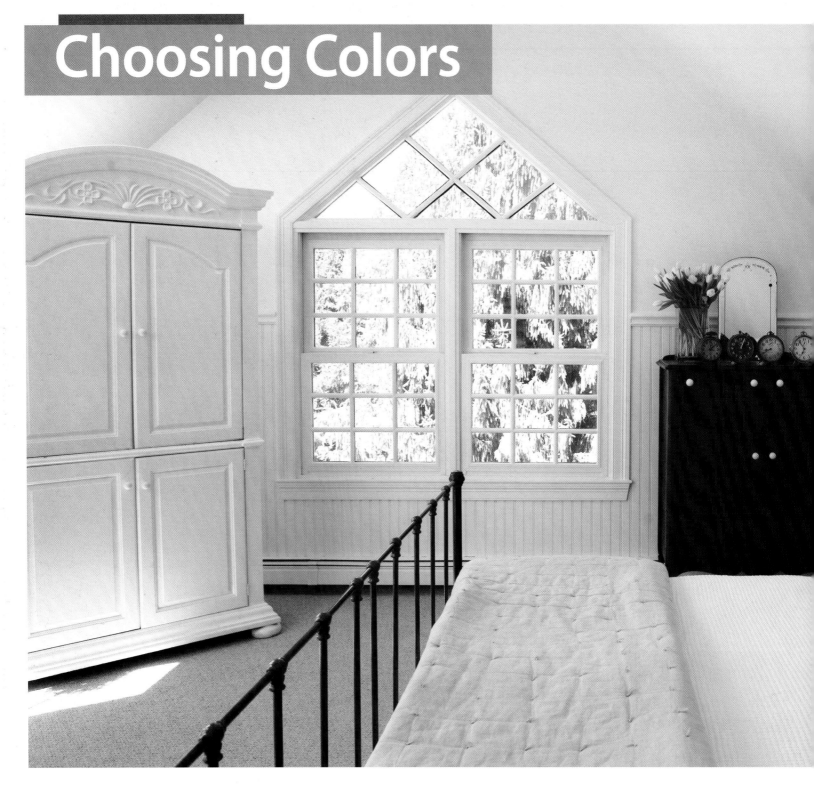

hoosing colors can be a somewhat scary proposition. Understanding some basic terminology and the principles of combining colors will help make the process easier.

Neutrals

True neutrals—white, black, and gray—play an essential role in decorating. Sometimes called "noncolors," true neutrals provide visual relief. A true neutral scheme depends on pattern, texture, and finish for visual interest.

White is the most popular of the true neutrals, but even white has variations of shade and subtlety. It is a standard backdrop for contemporary interiors, but it can also be solidly traditional. White heightens contrasts and adds depth and dimension to any room.

Black provides drama and definition to all elements of a space. Its anchoring quality can be used successfully in any design style. It can be overpowering, though, so use it judiciously. Gray, which is a mix of black and white, is softer than either of its parents. It's a good choice for a subtle neutral that

LEFT Sweet dreams can be had in this serene bedroom. White on white creates a sense of purity and peace.

ABOVE Black walls create drama and spaciousness in this multi-use living space.

RIGHT Perfect for reading or just getting away, this white room is a tranquil haven.

BELOW A living room full of soft neutral tones on the walls, cabinetry, and floor is a calm and relaxing space.

provides a clean canvas on walls and larger upholstered furniture, especially in an industrial design.

The "new" neutrals are low-intensity versions of colors, first made popular as sandy and taupe tones but now expanding into other colors. For example, if you lower the intensity of green as far as you can without losing all the color, you end up with a new-neutral green, just as you would if you added a small amount of green to a true gray. These quiet hues are ideal for walls and floors because they are low key, even when the color is spread over a large area.

True Colors

"Color is a powerful tool" according to paint specialists Virginia Young and Janie Lowe. "It can accentuate architectural details as well as direct traffic and create flow in your home. Blues are all about tranquility and relaxation; reds and rich earth tones are social-gathering colors. Choose your colors according to the use of the room and the mood you want to create."

The pure colors found on the color wheel aren't likely to be used in the home, but they are the basis of colors to use when decorating. Looking at a color wheel also can give you an idea of the types of colors you prefer, whether they are the warm reds and oranges of the left side of the wheel or the cooler blues and greens of the right side of the wheel.

The color wheels on this page show colors in a range of intensities—light, medium-light, medium, and dark. In reality, you will probably combine colors that vary in value and intensity, which will happen naturally when you use different materials.

Some color palettes are perennially popular. There will always be room for the tried-and-true classics such as blue-and-white kitchens and soft-green bedrooms. The emphasis on natural materials and finishes that are eco-friendly has increased the use of granite tones, greens, browns, and whites.

Ethnically influenced hues are also popular. The strong colors of Russian, Indian, and Latin design are mixing with more traditional European choices in both wall colors and fabrics to create exciting and modern blends.

Metallic paints and finishes are now found on everyday furniture, lighting, and accessories. These give a sensual and opulent feel to a room. Silver, gold, bronze, copper, and pearl add elegance without being too heavy. In daylight, these colors appear neutral; in the light of evening, they impart a welcoming glow to the room.

Saturated colors also glow more brightly, echoing the trends seen in technology and creating rich, interesting environments. Crystals, lacquer finishing, and sparkling textures are popular choices for plumbing and lighting.

OPPOSITE PAGE
Metallic bronze paint on a smooth wall finish provides a reflective backdrop for the plasma television and is a counterpoint for the stone fireplace below it.

Changing Colors

Color is never static. In today's world, it is more fluid than ever. It crosses geographic borders and defies time. Its influences come from a variety of global cultures. Fashions morph from runway to interiors in a heartbeat. The intersection of the 'green' movement and technology is blazing a new design path. Today's color palettes are taking on new shadings, and designers and consumers alike are ready to take on the new hues and combinations in their interior spaces."

Combining Colors

Individual colors are interesting, but the real fun happens when you bring colors together in a room. Endless color combinations are possible, but keep a few basic color principles in mind.

A monochromatic combination uses shades of a single color, and can be serene and elegant. The key to success is to use materials that are similar—but not identical—in lightness or darkness and in brightness or dullness. An analogous combination consists of colors that lie side by side on the color wheel, such as blue, blue-violet, and violet.

A complementary color combination is made up of colors that lie directly opposite each other on the color wheel, such as red and green. Approximately

opposite colors work well, too; for example, sage green (a yellow-green) pairs beautifully with violet. Sometimes combinations are more interesting when the colors are not direct opposites.

Complex color schemes consist of colors spread around the color wheel. You might choose colors that are equidistant on the color wheel, such as blue-green, red-violet, and yellow-orange. A four-color combination of equidistant colors is also possible, such as green, red, yellow-orange, and blue-violet. Complex color schemes automatically balance visually, but they can be a challenge to put together.

KEEP COLOR INTENSITY SIMILAR A room would be boring if all its colors

were the same intensity, but they should still work together. To keep one color from overwhelming the other colors in a space, make sure it isn't significantly darker or lighter than the others. In the same vein, use clear colors together and muted colors together. Even if colors are from opposite points on the color wheel, they will still feel harmonious.

BE AWARE OF UNDERTONES Most colors are mixtures of several colors, and the undertone, or underlying color, reflects that mix. The undertone will be either a warm color or a cool color. Your color choices will be more harmonious if all colors in the mix have the same type of undertone.

LEFT Colors galore fill this space, but the result is still harmonious. The green walls with white trim create a cool backdrop; yellow and gold fabrics and finishes provide warmth and contrast.

TOP LEFT Tone-on-tone gray elements provide a welcoming, natural feel. When in doubt, use a palette that ranges from the lightest shade of a color to the darkest.

TOP RIGHT Bold color can be added in small doses. Here, the color in the window coverings, blankets, and other elements enlivens the space.

BOTTOM Softer tones can be added in larger doses without overwhelming a room. The soft peach hues in this powder room are pleasing; a more intense orange shade would be oppressive.

USE UNEQUAL QUANTITIES Equal amounts of color fight for attention; unequal amounts are more pleasing. The secret is to let one color dominate while the others play supporting roles.

THINK ABOUT PLACEMENT Where you place colors in a room is just as important as using them in pleasing proportions. Even reversing the color choices between the walls and the furnishings, such as having lavender walls with yellow furnishings versus yellow walls with lavender furnishings, can make a difference in how you perceive the room. The visual impact of your decorating scheme is a direct result of color placement.

INTERIOR DESIGNER
KERRIE L. KELLY ON

Getting Started with Color

If you love the idea of strong hues but are afraid of the color commitment, you can always start with a neutral background and make the room shine by layering color on top in clear, bright strokes."

Color and Light

Light powerfully affects the perception of color. While most light in the home is artificial, natural light still plays an important role. The light in north-facing rooms tends to be cool, while south-facing rooms get inherently warmer light. To balance the "temperature" of the light in a room, use warm colors in north-facing rooms and cool colors in south-facing ones. Or enhance the natural temperature of a room with colors that match.

The way materials and surfaces reflect light also affects color. A shiny red lacquer table will reflect light and appear brighter, while the same red in a heavily textured fabric will be comparatively dull.

Color and Space

You can use colors to alter the perception of space within a room. Generally speaking, light colors give the illusion of more space while warm colors make a room seem smaller. Cool color tones and lighter colors make a room seem more open. More intense colors make a room seem smaller.

Color is also a useful tool to alter the apparent proportions of a room. Painting an end wall in a long, narrow room a warmer, darker color will help make the space feel more evenly proportioned. In a square room, painting one wall a more intense color than the other three walls can diminish the boxy look.

To create a smooth visual flow from room to room, use the same paint color and flooring throughout. To create a layered look and a sense of separation, use different colors in adjoining rooms. Or combine both approaches by choosing related but different colors for adjoining rooms.

PAINT SPECIALIST
JANIE LOWE ON

Interior Colors

"Color in architecture is a whole different animal than color in any other application. Because of the scale and the reflection of four walls on themselves, color becomes stronger in interior spaces. As a general rule, you should choose architectural colors that are more neutral than the end result you desire."

TOP The warm persimmon color in this living room, combined with the natural light from large windows, results in an inviting room in which to relax and entertain. The rich color is a good choice for this generously sized space.

BOTTOM LEFT A brightly colored wall and equally bright striped fabric draw attention to the breakfast area at the end of this galley kitchen.

BOTTOM RIGHT In this home, the kitchen walls provide a soothing contrast to the red dining room. White molding and the wood floor tie the two spaces together.

The sun shines even on cloudy mornings in this lovely dining room. Soft yellow provides a cheerful feeling while remaining neutral in tone.

Historical Hues

The depth of color on the walls is offset by the lighter tones on the ceilings and the neutral tones of the trim. The inside of the built-in hutch is lined with copper leaf, which adds a reflective quality.

OPPOSITE PAGE, TOP LEFT Because the kitchen walls are more than 12 feet high, the deep red ceiling (which could make a lower-ceilinged room feel closed in) is dramatic and warm.

OPPOSITE PAGE, TOP RIGHT The golden tone used on the entryway walls invites people into the house.

Built in 1888 as a Victorian farmhouse, this home reflects the passion for color shared by Yolo Colorhouse founders Janie Lowe and Virginia Young. The colors were chosen to emphasize the era's architectural style and to create a warm, inviting environment. The interior color palette is all about mood, exuding comfort and intimacy.

Not that Lowe and Young consider themselves done with the process of transformation. "Paint is the quickest and cheapest way to change the design of your house," Young says. "Our home is always evolving—that's what makes it exciting."

The Elements

■ **Ceilings:** The two color tones on the dining room ceiling draw attention to the fact that it's coved. Flat paint draws attention to the sheen of the walls, while the darker panel creates the illusion that the ceiling is higher than it actually is.

■ **Walls:** The wall colors reflect the landscape, bringing the outside in and creating warm living spaces during the cold, wet months in Portland, Oregon. The palette as a whole is designed to flow from one room to another.

■ **Trim:** Throughout the house, colored trim accentuates the character of the house and gives a nod to the original stained woodwork.

■ **Texture:** Clay plaster on the walls throughout the house creates an easy flow and adds a sheen that contrasts with the flat paint on the ceilings.

■ **Furnishings:** Furnishings throughout the house add another layer to the eclectic mix of color and architecture. The furniture is a collection of antiques and contemporary pieces, such as the Chermer chairs paired with a weathered picnic table.

Texture

The rustic brick wall is a classic textured surface. Here, a reclaimed door complements the wall's roughness, while the polished wood floor and dark chair play off the wall with their sleek surfaces.

Texture has the ability to add a powerful yet subtle dimension to a room's interior. It is one of the secret tools that design professionals use to make a strong impression within a space.

Most think texture is merely tactile. However, when you see something that feels rough, even though you may not touch it, your mind still knows how that object will feel. Using different textures allows you to affect the overall feeling of a room.

One of the basic principles of using texture involves perceived weight. Rough, coarse textures tend to make an object feel heavier, while smoother textures make it feel lighter. A polished white marble floor feels lighter than hardwood paneling, even though in actuality it is much heavier. When determining how much weight a certain texture adds to an item, the rule of thumb is that, generally, those objects that reflect more light tend to seem less heavy.

Fabrics, wall finishes, and flooring all add "actual" texture to a room. But you can also create "visual" texture. This can be done by sponge-painting a wall or upholstering a chair with a small-scale pattern, creating a play of light and shadow on a flat surface.

One common use of texture is to add interest to a space that uses monochromatic color schemes, such as shabby chic. In such a design, off-white walls are often adorned with elegant moldings and textured finishes, and are complemented by wicker and rattan, also painted white. The colors are the same, but the textures vary widely. No two colors match exactly, but they harmonize nicely.

Another example of effective use of textures can be found in rustic decor. In this style, rough walls and furnishings are matched with natural stone or wood floors and counters and thick shag carpets. Even though colors in this style are rich, with deep browns, blacks, and reds, it wouldn't feel like a rustic cabin style without the added depth.

Typically, historic decorating styles tend to be conservative. Texture is created by using mostly the same or similar tactile elements throughout a space. When contrasting sensations do exist, it is usually from two textures slowly melding into one another. Contemporary styles use texture more boldly. Modern decorative trends place rough unfinished brick next to stainless steel, or couple silk screens with concrete blocks.

Texture also affects color. Color on a smooth surface looks lighter than the same color on a textured surface. It is the subtle differences in color on different materials that help bring interest to a monochromatic room—no two elements match exactly, but they come together beautifully.

TOP LEFT Repeating the unique tile over the entire bathroom wall gives both actual and visual texture to the space.

TOP RIGHT A heavily textured wall makes this headboard the focus of the room while breaking up the large, solid dark walls.

BOTTOM A textured metallic wall covering defines the desk area of this office.

TOP LEFT A mix of silks, furs, and leather keeps this otherwise monochromatic bedroom lively.

BOTTOM LEFT The soft color palette on the walls and furniture is the perfect foil for the rich grouping of textures found in the organic fabrics and distressed woods and leathers used throughout this living room.

Working with Texture

Working different textures into a home decorating scheme is like combining patterns: Too much is unsettling but too little results in a dull room. Here are some points to consider.

BUILD ON WHAT IS THERE Start with the textures in your room's architecture, like a polished wood floor or the rough feel of an exposed brick wall. If you want similar textures, add complementary materials, such as silk draperies, to complement the floor. If you want more contrast, pair the floor with a textured carpet; the contrast may provide a pleasing difference.

MIX YOUR TEXTURES If your room decor is primarily mono-chromatic or neutral, introduce a variety of actual and visual textures to add interest to the space.

UNITE WITH COLOR Materials with wildly different textures work best together if they are all in the same color range.

ABOVE White is the primary color in the room, but the mix of textures, from the smooth couch to the wicker chairs and rough rug, keeps it from being boring.

All About Texture

White concrete was used to refinish the fireplace hearth; coral rock lines the façade.

TOP RIGHT A ripple-patterned MDF panel on the main wall replicates the way light shines on rippling water in nature. The depth of the textured wall and its shadows contrasts with the smooth white of the walls and porcelain fixtures, the sleek wood finishes, and the crisp chrome hardware.

BOTTOM RIGHT Milky-colored resin doors that open to the pool bath are punctuated with red saffron-like textural plant "threads." Light oak shelving with halogen lighting showcases clay and wooden bowls and holds guest towels.

Wayne Biemuller wanted his home to be light, airy, open, modern, and stylish. Texture was designer Susan Cozzi's solution. An edgy, stained-concrete floor was hand-troweled over existing tile and polished for a less industrial, more elegant look. The same concrete, only in white, was used to refinish the fireplace hearth. The furniture pieces are few but large, able to accommodate family and friends but also leaving wide pathways that contribute to a sense of spaciousness. A black coffee table with lots of grain anchors the space and adds drama.

The makeover continued in the master bath, with a strongly textured main wall, fixtures that appear to float, and specially designed resin doors. Tripling the amount of lighting throughout the house helps accent specific areas and adds to the overall light-and-airy feel.

The Elements

- **Flooring:** Stained and polished concrete, bamboo, and Plynyl were used throughout the house.

- **Lighting:** Halogen lights accent features and textures in all parts of the home.

- **Cabinetry:** The polished surface of the custom-stained oak contrasts nicely with the rougher textures in other areas.

- **Hardware:** Stainless steel and polished chrome are a perfect contrast to both the organic and more contemporary materials.

- **Finishing Touches:** Exotic wood bowls from American artisans and a Chinese bowl are featured; organic cotton used throughout maintains the natural feel of the space.

Pattern

Paisley fabric on the chairs coupled with a striped valance unify this seating area.

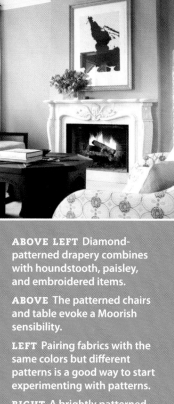

ABOVE LEFT Diamond-patterned drapery combines with houndstooth, paisley, and embroidered items.

ABOVE The patterned chairs and table evoke a Moorish sensibility.

LEFT Pairing fabrics with the same colors but different patterns is a good way to start experimenting with patterns.

RIGHT A brightly patterned wallpaper is the highlight of this bedroom.

Patterns are an integral part of the overall effect of a room. Patterns on fabrics are the most obvious usage, but there are also inherent patterns in furniture shapes and their placement. A successful mix of patterns results in a balanced and beautiful room. But it takes a deft hand. Too much use of patterns and the room appears over-powering; too little and the room is bland. It's more than just mixing and matching colors. The trick is to find just the right combination of scale and design to create the perfect effect.

STYLE Patterns come in many different styles. Naturalistic patterns are realistic renderings of natural forms, such as flowers and birds. Stylized patterns simplify natural designs to capture their essence; the fleur-de-lis, for example, is a stylized iris. Geometric designs include stripes, checks, and plaids. Abstract patterns are loose artistic interpretations of realistic or geometric designs.

SCALE The scale of a pattern is determined by the size of its motifs or designs. Small-scale patterns can read as texture and can be a place for the eye to rest when used with larger patterns. Medium-scale patterns are versatile and seldom overpower other elements. With large-scale patterns, which work well in generously proportioned rooms, make sure you have a large enough area to display several pattern repeats so the design does not look truncated.

Combining Patterns

Thinking about how patterns interact makes the job of choosing and combining patterns easier. And looking at the way professional designers combine patterns with great flair—often defying rules while doing so—will offer inspiration. Following are some guidelines that will help.

TIE PATTERNS TOGETHER Take the one pattern you are most attracted to as your inspiration. Choose two or more that work with it. Three patterns provide plenty of variety; more than three can be overwhelming.

USE COLOR TO UNIFY Patterns with light backgrounds open up a room. Those with dark backgrounds make it more intimate.

VARY THE PATTERNS Choose a variety of styles and use patterns that are different in scale. For example, try a large-scale plaid with a medium-scale leaf pattern and a small-scale stripe that combines the colors from both.

KEEP YOUR ROOM IN MIND While choosing patterns, think about where they will be placed. The medium-scale leaf pattern may be used for the draperies and repeated on the sofa's accent pillows. The small stripe on the sofa may be complemented by the large-scale plaid on the ottoman.

Playful Yet Elegant

The great room's taupe-striped walls echo in the rug and throw pillows. Red floors, chairs, and accessories keep the space lively.

RIGHT The stairway's yellow bands run horizontally, setting off the naturally vertical space and highlighting the colors in the framed jerseys.

Bold stripes are graphic, clean, modern, and fun. As a design motif, though, they're more apt to be associated with a circus. But when the owners of this cottage requested a look that was "happy and playful," designer Michel Biehn says, "We went crazy with stripes and kept going."

The trick was to incorporate the pattern seamlessly into the walls, floors, furnishings, textiles, and accessories, and balance it with neutrals for an eye-catching—not dizzying—result. "It's a delicate combination of elegance and wit," Biehn adds.

The Elements

■ **Floors:** The hardwood floors throughout are finished with a water-based tomato red, which forms the core of the entire palette and is reflected in the red accents used on the chairs and accessories.

■ **Motif:** Stripes are used throughout the house, but by varying the color, width, direction, and materials, they don't seem overdone.

■ **Visual Links:** The sisal rug in the main room is trimmed to match the floor; the yellow stripes in the hall pick up the yellow hues of the framed sports jerseys.

Chapter 5

Furniture

More than anything else, the furniture you choose will define the style of your room. It is the dominant feature. The backdrops—walls, flooring, colors—can work with a number of decorating approaches. Furniture, on the other hand, has an unmistakably specific style and design. In this chapter, you'll learn about how good-quality furniture is constructed and what to look for in upholstered pieces, as well as gather ideas for reusing existing pieces in new ways.

Furniture Basics

Furniture style choices are endless. You may prefer the elegance of traditional furniture, the casualness of beach-house decor, or the clean lines of modern styling. But no matter which style of furniture you prefer, understanding its relative quality is essential. Furniture in any price range is a good value only when the quality of the materials and construction is in line with the price. Consequently, it's important to have some knowledge of materials and construction to make wise furniture selections.

Furniture designer Michael Hennessey believes, "The product has to last. Not only in utility, but in beauty, too, a product has to have a reason to be passed along instead of thrown away. A product that is created from real wood, incorporates timeless design, and has simple inner beauty will be passed along to friends or relatives or even sold in a garage sale. Whatever the case, the lifecycle is greatly extended by these simple principles."

LEFT Upholstered pieces, wicker, and reclaimed wood all work together in this combination living and dining room—proof that you don't need to stick to just one furniture style to make a statement.

TOP RIGHT A painted wood cocktail table, custom-made swinging sofa, and leather sectional combine to create a Cuban atmosphere that evokes the home-owner's vacation memories.

BOTTOM RIGHT Luxurious Italian leather and a substantial yet elegant chrome frame are indicators of both the high style and overall quality of this chaise.

Take your time when looking for furniture. It's usually a large purchase, and one you will probably have for a considerable length of time. Learn what appeals to you personally. And don't be afraid to mix and match different styles. A room with a blend of pieces that appeal to the homeowner is inherently more interesting than one that resembles a furniture showroom. But no matter what you choose, it's important that the pieces be of good quality and will last.

Wooden Furniture

Furniture craftsmen have used wood for thousands of years. It is strong yet easy to cut, carve, join, finish, and refinish. Caring for it is relatively simple, and when pieces are well made and maintained, they improve with age. Wood is also an environmentally friendly, renewable resource. Because it was once part of a living organism, wood has warmth and appeal.

Hardwoods come from deciduous trees, such as oak, pecan, walnut, birch, maple, mahogany, and cherry. These woods have tighter grains that make them stronger, denser, and a better choice for carving and detailing. Softwoods, from cone-bearing trees or conifers, include pine, cedar, cypress, spruce, fir, and redwood. The grain of softwoods is more open in appearance. Softwood pieces are typically less expensive.

A number of terms are used to describe wooden furniture. Understanding what they mean will help you when you're shopping. The term *all-wood construction* means that the visible parts of the piece are made of wood. *Combination* indicates that more than one type of wood makes up the piece's exposed parts. The word *solid* means that a solid piece of wood was used for construction.

Veneer is a thin slice of beautifully grained wood that has been bonded to plywood or particleboard. Though many think of veneer as the result of a modern construction method, veneers have been used for centuries to create pieces of great beauty and strength. *Genuine* indicates that veneers of a particular wood were placed over hardwood plywood on all exposed parts of the piece.

FURNITURE DESIGNER
MICHAEL HENNESSEY ON

Caring for Wood Furniture

To ensure the long life and beauty of wood furniture, avoid excessive sunlight, dampness, heat, or cold. Place a felt or leather pad under all lamp bases and accessories to avoid surface scratches. Polish only every six months with a silicone-free polish; polishing too often may result in a waxy buildup. For routine cleaning, use a cloth that has been dampened with a diluted cleaning polish. Clean spills or smudges with a damp cloth moistened in mild soap or cleaning polish."

OPPOSITE PAGE, TOP
The carved detail gives this dining chair its Asian-influenced style.

OPPOSITE PAGE, BOTTOM Crafted in a high-gloss Palisander finish with metal and glass accents, this double pedestal desk and efficient credenza will suit any workaholic with designer style.

TOP LEFT One of the advantages of wood is that it can be painted, and repainted, to match any decor.

TOP RIGHT These Asian-style saddleback stools are a perfect example of how wood gives even the simplest design a feeling of richness, warmth, and quality.

LEFT A rectangular table made of Macassar ebony with black lacquer accents is paired with black upholstered chairs.

Joining Methods

One of the most important considerations when selecting furniture is how the pieces were joined together. A number of joining methods are in use, all of which have their advantages.

One of the oldest and strongest methods of joinery is a mortise and tenon, which is formed by two pieces of wood that interlock. Mitered joints or corners, in turn, are formed when two pieces of wood meet at a 45-degree angle. Mitered joints must be reinforced with screws, dowels, metal splines, or nails. Pieces can also be connected by dowels that are glued into predrilled holes. The quality of this type of joint relies on the strength of the dowel.

Dovetail joints are used to secure drawer fronts and sides. This joint takes its name from a series of notches carved into one of the pieces and the matching projections that are on the other piece.

Corner blocks are triangular pieces of wood that are glued and screwed into place at an angle. These blocks act as reinforcements at stress points, such as where table tops meet the legs.

RIGHT Mortise-and-tenon joinery adds strength to this stool.

Quality Check

When you're buying wood furniture, check that each piece meets the following guidelines to be sure it is well made.

- ☐ Doors and drawers should fit tightly without sticking.
- ☐ Drawers should slide easily on glides or ball bearings.
- ☐ Drawer interiors should be smooth and free from splinters.
- ☐ Pieces should have strong joinery and corner blocks.
- ☐ Back panels and dust panels should be secure between drawers.
- ☐ Sanding and finishing should be smooth on unexposed surfaces.
- ☐ Hardware should be of good quality.
- ☐ Exterior finishes should be clear and without defects.

LEFT Built-in details are indicators of higher-end construction.

ABOVE Veneered exotic woods are an indication of the quality of workmanship in this chest; the flip-top mirror adds functionality.

Metal Furniture

Like wood, metal has been used for furniture construction for thousands of years. It has great durability and strength and can be formed into limitless shapes. Because of its durability and aesthetic flexibility, metal can be used in almost any decor.

Certain metals, however, have proven to be reliable choices. Others, such as chromium or chrome, are generally used for plating; still others, such as silver, gold, pewter, bronze, copper, and tin, are used for finishing,

Iron is one of the most popular metal choices for furniture. It is both strong and durable. Brass, formed from zinc and copper, can be used either by itself or as plating for furniture and accessories. While steel is stronger than iron, it's not usually used in homes. Stainless steel is often used for furniture hardware and fittings rather than for furniture itself.

Metal furniture can be found in a range of quality and price points. The quality of metal pieces depends on their construction. Metal furniture components should fit together tightly. The finish should be smooth and free of imperfections.

LEFT Simple metal tubing provides the framing for this cushioned sofa.

RIGHT A stainless steel table with matching chairs is a nice counterpoint to the warm wood used elsewhere in this kitchen.

TOP LEFT Ideal for patios and porches, wicker adds lightness to a space.

BOTTOM LEFT A rattan headboard and footboard coupled with metals and wood carvings turn a standard bed into a plantation-inspired four-poster.

BOTTOM RIGHT Rush seats and a coordinating sisal floor rug soften this outdoor table setting.

OPPOSITE PAGE A French antique wooden dining table takes on fresh appeal when paired with colorful plastic-and-metal chairs.

CANE is made from grasses, palm stems, or plants such as rattan or bamboo. Thin strips of these materials are woven into a mesh and fitted into the back or seat of a furniture frame. The mesh enables ventilation. Cane is surprisingly strong while still having "give" for comfort.

RUSH is a long grass that is twisted to form a thin cord for weaving chair seats. It is also used for area rugs. Rush is a strong and long-lasting material.

Natural Materials

Furniture made from wicker, rattan, cane, and rush adds a natural feeling to any room. It is also surprisingly versatile, fitting in well with a number of decorating styles.

WICKER is not a specific material, but rather the term that identifies a furniture piece made from the combination of small twigs and flexible wood strips. It's a natural for porches and sunrooms,

and is often found in Victorian and beach-style decor.

RATTAN is made from the unbranched stem of the Indian palm used to make wicker furniture. Rattan poles are flexible and can be bent, stained, lacquered, painted, nailed, or screwed, unlike bamboo, which is brittle and hollow. Though most people associate rattan with outdoor and tropical settings, it adds a soft warmth to any space.

Plastic Furniture

The plastics most commonly used for interior furnishings include vinyl, polyurethanes, acrylics, and melamine or laminates. These materials add a fun and modern feel to any room, and can be a good choice for family rooms and play areas. However, plastics can be highly flammable and give off poisonous gases or fumes when burned. Always follow the manufacturer's instructions for care.

Upholstered Furniture

The quality of fabric-covered furniture is often difficult to assess, because you cannot see how it is constructed. Still, it is worthwhile to take the time to learn about the basics so you can find pieces that are good quality and a good value.

FRAME CONSTRUCTION Frames for upholstered furniture are made from the same materials as case goods: wood, metal, and plastic. Wooden frames should be made of hardwood to ensure strength. They should be secured with double dowels and glue, and the corners should be blocked, braced, and screwed into place.

COILS AND SPRINGS Springs are composed of either coils or sinuous wire. Coil springs are attached to a tightly woven webbing of rubber and metal, linen, jute, or a synthetic material. The webbing is stretched across and attached to the bottom of the frame and serves as a base. Each spring is tied together at the top in at least eight places.

Sinuous wire, or no-sag springs, is made from a single wire that is bent in a continuously curved zigzag and attached to the frame. This type of spring is used in chair backs or upholstered pieces with thin profiles because it requires less space than traditional springs.

CUSHIONING A layer of burlap protects and supports padding and keeps it from working into the springs. The padding is typically made of a soft layer of cotton or polyester batting. Padding covers the springs and frame and gives shape and form to an upholstered furniture piece. A casing of muslin holds padding in place and protects it from the fabric covering.

Loose cushions can be filled with down and feathers, foam, fiberfill, or a combination of these materials. Down is considered the most luxurious and expensive of fillers and is distinguished by its soft, casual look. Because down and feathers are not resilient, these cushions require frequent plumping.

The most common cushioning is polyurethane foam with a wrapping of polyester batting. This type of cushioning comes in a variety of densities and is nonallergenic, resilient, and impervious to moisture. Polyester fiberfill adds softness, resiliency, and comfort to the cushion.

Reversible cushions extend the life of an upholstered piece, and should be turned periodically.

OPPOSITE PAGE A sectional with bolstered arms and extra-wide chaise is comfortable and versatile. The two-tier glass and stainless cocktail table allows homeowners to display an array of collectibles of varying heights.

Quality Check

When looking for upholstered furniture, you'll need to look at both the frame construction and the upholstery materials. Consider these points before buying.

☐ Be sure the fabric pattern and nap (the direction of the pile) match.

☐ Look for smooth seams and straight welts or covered cording without puckers.

☐ Verify that cushions fit properly.

☐ Be aware of loose or hanging threads.

☐ Check to see that buttons are tight on tufted pieces.

☐ Check quilting if applicable and ensure it was done well.

TOP These wood frames are inset with microfiber, which is both beautiful and durable.

BOTTOM Adding a cushioned and upholstered pillowtop gives an heirloom look to this modern cocktail table.

Choosing Fabrics

When it comes to interior design, the right fabric can enhance your design aesthetically in a way no other component can come close to. Interior designer Jennifer Hilgardner says, "Find a fabric you love. Choose a signature fabric with enough design elements so that you can pull out colors, coordinate textures, and have lots of options for furnishings and accessories."

Identical pieces covered in dissimilar fabrics will have a very different finished appearance. Tone and texture differences can vary appearances as well. Since the cover is such a visible part of the piece, it is typically a major influence in the design selection process.

Consider first a fabric's suitability. A lighter-weight fabric may be fine for a seldom-used piece. For pieces that get more constant use, such as those in a family room, you need something that is more durable. Look at stain-resistant options, especially if you have children or pets. Leather is a popular choice for couches and chairs.

LEFT Shades of green with blue and brown accents play off the tropical foliage seen through the picture windows.

RIGHT Simple styling, full cushions, and welting detail are key indicators of the quality of this sofa.

To ensure the long life and beauty of any upholstered piece, avoid excessive sunlight, dampness, heat, or cold. Hand fluff and reverse cushions regularly to maintain their original softness and resiliency. Vacuum to remove all surface dust. Spot-clean any spills immediately; start with water before using chemicals.

Natural Fabrics

Cotton, linen, silk, and wool have been the staples of upholstery for generations. Each has its pros and cons.

COTTON is stable and durable; resists moths, abrasion, and static; and comes in a wide range of weights, textures, and patterns. It will fade and rot in the sun and can mildew. Untreated, it will wrinkle and shrink during cleaning.

LINEN is strong and durable, and resists static, moths, soil, and sun rot, though it will fade in the sun. Linen wrinkles unless blended with more stable fibers, such as cotton or polyester. It can also stretch or shrink in humid climates.

SILK is long lasting if handled carefully. It resists abrasion and moths. But it will fade and rot in the sun, and can mildew, wrinkle, and pick up static electricity.

WOOL is a durable fiber that is most stable if blended with synthetics. It will fade and rot in the sun. It also reacts to humidity and temperature changes, picks up static electricity, pills, and must be treated to resist moths and mildew.

Synthetic Fibers

Synthetic fibers are coming into their own. They often combine the best features of natural fabrics. Their quality, too, has improved over the years. Choices include acetate, acrylic, nylon, polyester, and rayon.

INTERIOR DESIGNER
KERRIE L. KELLY ON

Caring for Leather

To ensure the long life and beauty of leather pieces, simply dust lightly with a soft, dry cloth and occasionally touch up with leather conditioner."

Repurposing Furniture

Used furniture usually does not come in sets. Don't be afraid to mix and match. Choose pieces with the same general shape and materials for a cohesive yet eclectic look.

Furniture that's no longer needed for its original use can have a second life serving an entirely new function. Experts call this "repurposing" furniture. Use repurposed furniture to add an element of the unexpected to a room.

Interior designer Jennifer Hilgardner says, "A dresser is one of the best examples of repurposing furniture because it is one of the most universal pieces. I have used dressers in entryways—a tray on top gathers keys and mail, and drawers capture hats, gloves, scarves, and mittens." Other repurposed ideas include a dresser or buffet in a workroom to store art supplies and in a kitchen for pots and pans. "A small dresser with drawers can be used just about anywhere," Hilgardner adds.

Changing Faces

It just takes imagination, and maybe some simple fixes, to change the function of a piece of furniture. Adding a granite or butcher-block top can make a dresser just right in the kitchen. Changing knobs and hinges can give furniture a whole new look. And if you want a bigger challenge, you can transform furniture completely by staining the wood a different color or sanding and painting it.

Perhaps the latest furniture piece being given a second life is the giant television armoire. Modern flat-screen and plasma TVs are turning these armoires into relics, but they don't have to be. Furniture designer Michael Hennessey points out, "Selling your older furniture pieces is not going to get you a lot of money. So get creative and change the purpose for a functional use in another area of your home."

With some adjustments—removing the doors, replacing wood shelves with glass, and adding a mirror as a backdrop—an old armoire can become a wine cabinet. Or it can be repurposed into a home office, with storage for a computer and drawer space for paper and a printer. With repurposing, the choices are limitless.

ABOVE Repurposed lockers with a fresh coat of red paint serve as additional storage at the top of the stairs.

RIGHT A chest normally found in a hallway or dining room becomes the perfect storage piece for towels and toiletries in a bathroom.

BELOW An 1887 tavern table coupled with an old card catalog now make up the island in this kitchen.

FURNITURE DESIGNER
MICHAEL HENNESSEY ON

Changing Furniture Nomenclature

Don't be afraid of breaking an unspoken design rule or to remove the name of the furniture from its purpose. Just because it's called a dining room hutch doesn't mean it needs to reside in a dining room."

For the Long Haul

Mahogany furniture is a good match for the distressed hardwood flooring. The head chairs are upholstered in a creamy linen that complements the leather used on the side chairs.

OPPOSITE PAGE, TOP A contemporary painting, rather than the expected collection of matching French pieces, sets off this buffet. An artist was commissioned to paint several pieces for this home.

OPPOSITE PAGE, BOTTOM LEFT Traditional chairs flank this stately fireplace.

OPPOSITE PAGE, BOTTOM RIGHT A custom hand-carved pool table with a custom finish and dark felt harkens back to a traditional pool-hall look.

When Jason and Jill Williams hired design firm All American Design & Furnishings to design their home, they clearly stated that the theme was "sparse." They did not intend to buy things to simply fill the house. Instead, they wanted to acquire pieces over time that had meaning and use and that complemented their lifestyle and reflected their personality.

This meant that every piece they purchased would have a purpose. While their theme was "sparse," sleek and modern wasn't their design choice. Instead, they wanted a mix of furniture styles with rustic, stained, and painted finishes. The result: a combination of traditional and painted furniture. Every piece serves a purpose, and each can be used in different ways for years to come.

The Elements

- **Dining Room Chairs:** The distressed mahogany chairs are upholstered in a mix of leather and cream linen with nailheads.

- **Dining Room Table:** A rectangular distressed table with an inlaid design includes details such as the Xs at the top of each tapered leg and a furniture-style drawer at each end for storage.

- **Drapery:** Thai silk floor-to-ceiling tone-on-tone lined fabric provides softness while framing the home's views. The banded bottom adds interest and works well with the hardwood flooring.

- **Artwork:** Commissioned artwork expresses the homeowner's personality while adding color and texture to the room.

- **Pool Table:** The handmade pool table looks more like furniture; the coordinating pool-stick holder ties into the hardwood floor.

- **Buffet:** A custom-finish buffet provides storage behind closed doors and accents the artwork.

Chapter 6

Finishing Touches

The finishing touches are what turn a beautifully designed room into a room with a distinct personality. Lighting is a key component; choosing the right fixtures and bulbs and using them effectively are essential to making a room inviting and comfortable. Accessories—ranging from mirrors and pillows to artwork, photographs, and personal mementos—ensure that the space is uniquely yours. And don't overlook storage. It's always needed, and options range from display shelving to pieces that are beautiful furnishings in their own right.

Lighting Basics

OPPOSITE PAGE A hanging fixture coupled with recessed can lights on dimmers provides the ultimate versatility for this nook.

RIGHT Ceiling-hung lights with personality can do double duty as art. A one-of-a-kind light fixture customizes any room.

How a room is lit affects the overall impression of the space: The right lighting can add drama and elegance to a room. The ideal lighting scheme is natural light supplemented with ambient, task, and accent lighting. Lighting specialist Zack Rosson says, "The combination of lighting and sunlight can completely change the feeling of a home. A balanced mix of the two sustains the warmth of a room while allowing homeowners to create different moods."

Ambient, or general, lighting sets the room's mood. The even glow fills the space and makes it more inviting by eliminating harsh shadows. Ambient lighting is usually provided by indirect fixtures such as shaded lamps, overhead lighting, and chandeliers, though it can also be achieved with directional fixtures aimed at a wall or built-in lighting in a cove or cornice.

Task lighting is the bright light that illuminates a particular area in which an activity takes place—reading, playing games, or preparing food, for example. The pattern of light is focused tightly onto a specific space, and its sharper pool of light often contrasts pleasantly with overall ambient light. Task lighting must be adjustable and able to be shielded. It's best to aim task lighting at an angle to avoid hot spots or shadows.

Accent lighting includes the most romantic light, which comes from the flicker of candles. Nothing is better at inducing conversation or creating an intimate mood. Accent lighting is also used to highlight features, such as artwork or architectural elements, or to provide a sense of drama. The beam spread, intensity, and color are important considerations when choosing accent lighting.

The best lighting schemes combine these three different types of lighting without overusing any of them. Finding the right mix can be tricky, but is worth the time and effort. Using too many lights or high-wattage bulbs can wash out a room's beauty, while insufficient lighting can create a room that is cold and uninviting.

LEFT A contemporary table is paired with a new take on a traditional chandelier. Uplighting, rather than direct downlights, ensures there will be no glare when dining.

RIGHT A mix of lighting is key to illuminating this room. During the day, floor-to-ceiling windows provide natural light. Floor lamps by the chair and couch provide ambient and task lighting. Over the table, pendant lights provide sufficient illumination for dining or board games.

Creating a Lighting Scheme

Layering is the key to creating a lighting scheme that is balanced. First, identify the main activity areas or the room's focal points and put the brightest layer of light there. Next, create a middle layer to highlight interest in specific areas without detracting from the focal points. A third layer fills in the background. The first two layers require task or accent lighting; the last needs ambient light.

GETTING CONTROL One of the best, and least expensive, ways to control lighting is with dimmers, also called rheostats. Dimmers not only can set a mood, but also will conserve energy. They also help you custom-tailor light in a room for multiple uses and decorative effects.

Another option is a control panel. Lighting controls give you the flexibility to design a lighting plan with many uses and a variety of decorative touches. With the push of a button, you can use today's sophisticated dimming systems to lower light levels to conserve energy and increase bulb life, alter the intensity of light to suit the activity, and create and save a number of different lighting scenes in each room.

BEWARE OF GLARE When placing light fixtures, consider the glare they produce. Direct glare from a bare bulb is the worst kind. Remedies include deeply recessed fixtures, fixtures with black baffles or small apertures, clip-on louvers and shutters, silvered-bowl bulbs, and diffusing shades or covers. You can avoid reflected glare by placing fixtures at a 30- to 45-degree angle.

Choosing Lighting Sources

You would think that choosing light fixtures comes first, but professional designers pick bulbs—which they call "lamps"—and then the appropriate fixtures. Bulbs and tubes can be grouped according to the way they produce light.

INCANDESCENT BULBS These produce a warm light that flatters skin tones. They can be controlled by dimmers and three-way switches. Incandescent bulbs can be used as ambient, task, or accent lighting.

HALOGEN BULBS These give off the whitest light and do not change interior color perception. They are ideal for task and accent lighting. They must be used in halogen fixtures only.

FLUORESCENT BULBS These create a steady, shadowless light, said to simulate daylight. They are highly energy efficient, and come in both tubes and bulbs. The newest generation of fluorescent bulbs has minimal noise and flicker, and comes in a wide spectrum of colors.

COMPACT FLUORESCENT LIGHT BULBS CFLs use 70 percent less energy than the incandescent light bulbs that they

replace. They're available in various sizes and shapes to match different fixtures, and come in different shades of white light. You can even find CFLs for use with a dimmer switch or a three-way fixture.

OTHER LIGHT SOURCES Some specialty lights don't provide a great deal of useful light but can be fun as decorative elements. These include neon, fiber-optic, and rope lights.

GENERAL CONTRACTOR
JOHN SLAUGHTER ON

Lights for Small Spaces

Install jamb switches that automatically turn on the lights in closets and cabinets when the door is open. This easy fix will make it much easier to find items quickly in these often poorly lit spaces."

task, and accent lighting and let you move them whenever you want. Small specialty lamps, such as clip-on lights, uplight cans, adjustable task lights, mini-reflector spotlights, desk lamps, and piano lamps, provide task and accent lighting.

Lighting specialist Zack Rosson says, "Hot lamp trends include clear- and colored-glass bases, designs in ceramic and porcelain, and table lamps with designer lampshades. When shopping for shades, look for color on the exterior of the shade and fabulous pattern on the interior of the shade for extra personality."

OVERHEAD FIXTURES These lights include ceiling fixtures, chandeliers, track lighting, and recessed lighting. Ceiling fixtures provide general lighting. They are practical in busy areas such as foyers, hallways, bedrooms, kitchens, baths, laundry rooms, playrooms, and dens.

Chandeliers are often a source of mood lighting. They create ambience within the room, either by varying the color or the intensity of the light emitted or by the style of the fixture itself. A five-arm wrought-iron chandelier is a traditional look, while a crystal chandelier is opulent, exuding an air of elegance and sophistication. Candle chandeliers are soft and romantic; an antler chandelier is a decidedly more rustic look. Some chandeliers even include downlights for task lighting. Never hesitate to use a chandelier in any room—including in an office or in a bedroom. It is the perfect unexpected accent that packs a lot of drama.

Pendants, equipped with shades or globes to prevent glare, are generally suspended over tables, islands, or other work areas, and can provide both task and ambient lighting. When used over end or night tables, they free up the space occupied by table lamps.

Track lighting can provide ambient, task, or accent lighting all in one flexible lighting system. You can move, swivel, rotate, and aim the individual fixtures in any direction along the track. You can also hang chandeliers and pendants from the track.

Recessed lighting also provides general, task, or accent lighting, and is less conspicuous than track lighting. Recessed fixtures can be used anywhere in the home, including outdoors under eaves. They are ideal for low-ceiling areas, and, with a special adapter, they can also be used in cathedral ceilings. They are available as downlights, adjustable accent lights, and wall washers.

OTHER CHOICES Sconces light the perimeter of a room, expanding the space visually. Older and historic homes often include sconce fixtures. In today's newer homes, the high windows, walls, and soaring ceilings increase the need for

Choosing Fixtures

Given the great variety of light fixtures available today, finding the right ones can be overwhelming. A primary consideration is how the fixture directs light—whether it's narrow and focused or broad and diffused—so match the type of light distribution to the lighting need: task lighting for reading, overall ambient light for watching television.

Be sure the fixture is an appropriate size for the room; fixtures often look smaller in lighting showrooms, so bring measurements. Fixtures used in kitchens, bathrooms, and work areas should be easy to clean. The best choices for fixtures in hard-to-reach areas such as above the stairs are those that take long-lived fluorescent or halogen bulbs.

LAMPS The traditional lamp is still incredibly versatile and practical in both style and use. Lamps can provide ambient,

OPPOSITE PAGE, TOP A floor lamp is often the perfect choice for a living room. It provides enough light for reading, and adds a warm glow to the space.

OPPOSITE PAGE, BOTTOM LEFT Drum-style pendants are versatile in any type of interior. Here, the pendant illuminates the space over a staircase, acting as both lighting and a design accent.

OPPOSITE PAGE, BOTTOM RIGHT This pendant fixture offers a fresh alternative to the typical bedside lamp.

RIGHT Wall sconces flanking framed bathroom mirrors create an elegant feel while providing additional light for makeup application and shaving.

FAR RIGHT, TOP Undercabinet lighting provides additional illumination in kitchen work areas.

FAR RIGHT, BOTTOM Candelabras and a candlelit chandelier create a welcome setting in this dining room.

supplemental lighting, and sconces are an ideal solution. They are also highly decorative, including some that mimic candles and others that are created from hand-blown glass.

Undercabinet fixtures are used for both task and accent lighting. When placed under kitchen cabinets, they light the countertop; in a display cabinet, they show off prized possessions. They're also popular for workshops or other spaces in which you need lighting right at hand. Choices include slim, energy-efficient fluorescents; miniature track lighting; and strips of low-voltage mini-lights.

Vanity light bars, primarily used in bathrooms, supply task lighting that's ideal for applying makeup, shaving, and grooming while supplementing the general lighting provided by ceiling fixtures.

Candlelight is the oldest artificial light source. Its warmth creates a quiet and private atmosphere and softens the edges of a hectic day. From tea lights surrounding a tub to pillar candles atop burnished copper plates in a living room, candlelight is dramatic, effective, and stylish.

LIGHTING SPECIALIST ZACK ROSSON ON

Caring for Light Fixtures

To maintain fixtures' beauty, all finishes should be wiped gently with a soft, damp cloth, followed by a soft, dry cloth. Avoid cleansers with ammonia, bleach, or harsh chemicals. Silk and velum shades should be brushed gently with a feather duster or soft cloth to remove surface dust."

The final details you add to a room are what set it apart. Some are obvious additions: pillows, throws, mirrors, and artwork. More subtle items might be books, photos, plants, or personal collections. Still others are treasured keepsakes, whether family treasures, mementos from special occasions or special people, or souvenirs from vacations. All impart a personal quality to the living space.

The advantage of these final touches is that they're flexible. You can have different pillows for different seasons, add or subtract throw rugs and photos, or bring in plants in bloom and then return them to the garden when they finish their display. You can always add and subtract. And if you don't like the result, you can always rearrange.

Most of all, make sure you like all the things you display and that they have meaning for you.

Elements of Display

No matter what objects you include in a room, some basic design rules will help keep the result cohesive. Start by looking for a visual connection. It might be a common color element, either in the pieces themselves or the backdrop they are displayed against.

Also, think about different levels. Include both tall and low elements throughout the room to keep your eye moving. If you place items on a flat surface, such as a dresser or shelves, don't just line them up. Instead, treat them as a still life, using them to tell a story about the people in the house. When possible, give the display a high point and let the side support pieces trail from it, creating an overall triangle effect.

As a general rule, hang framed photos and artwork at eye level or a bit higher if the ceilings are high, for greater impact. Or, try a modern way to display your art collection: Lean multiple frames of various sizes and finishes against the wall on a floating shelf for a chic collage effect. Feel free to combine photos, paintings, drawings, and maps—they tell more of a story when mixed. With a little creativity, it is easy to transform a single wall into your own personal gallery.

Finally, don't overlook the unexpected element. Add a zebra rug to a formal living room or include an elaborate silver teapot in a room filled with contemporary chrome-finished furniture. The trick is to add unexpected pieces in small doses, to keep them from overwhelming the rest of the space.

OPPOSITE PAGE A lipstick-red wall sets off black-and-white photos and a mix of collected treasures.

ABOVE Use a common color scheme and a grid of frames to unite children's drawings for a singular display.

RIGHT A small artifact collection is set off by the white backdrop. By arranging the pieces in a loose triangle, the overall effect appears harmonious but not overly formal.

Adding in Details

There are no hard-and-fast rules to follow when deciding what you want in a room. Perhaps you favor a clean, minimalist look. In that case, just a simple orchid and an oversize art book might be all you want on a coffee table. Or maybe you're more comfortable with things you love surrounding you. In that case, the same coffee table might be filled with photos, books and magazines, a teapot and teacup, several plants, and a favorite piece found while traveling. It's all up to you, but here are some ideas for finishing off a room in style.

PILLOWS Pillows are a great way to change the look of your room. You can get a custom look by adding fabric or other details to a ready-made pillow. For true personalization, have a pillow monogrammed—use script lettering for a formal setting or block letters for a more relaxed look. Scattering pillows of the same color throughout your house is a great way to create a flow of color. Custom floor pillows can provide extra seating for kids and adults.

MIRRORS In large rooms, mirrors add to the grandeur of the space. In small rooms, a reflective surface makes the room feel larger and more airy, creating an illusion of depth. Rectangular versions add volume and height, while square versions add symmetry. If you have crooked ceilings or asymmetrical walls, bold frames distract from their irregularities while adding character.

BOOKS If you love to read, books can quickly overtake a space. And for good reason: Not only are they decorative, for a true bookworm they're comforting. The sheer volume, though, can be overwhelming. Try to add some visual space to a bookshelf, either with other objects or simply by turning the books on their sides. If you don't have the proper space to display books in a bookcase, you can respectfully use them as doorstops and end tables.

PHOTOGRAPHS Unify a collection of prints of different sizes and subjects by framing them in the same way, or display mixed-frame works inside three-dimensional shadow boxes. Hung together on a wall, these groupings take the place of one large piece of art.

SPECIAL COLLECTIONS A collection is probably the most personal addition to any space. The choices are endless: china, pottery, glassware, lithographs and prints, even old-fashioned flour and sugar canisters can be displayed.

FAMILY HISTORY One of the most meaningful additions to any room is something that tells your family history. It may be a grandfather clock or a pocket watch; family silver or your grandmother's old brown teapot; books, photos, or a child's toy handed down from generation to generation.

GLOBAL INFLUENCES Souvenirs you collect on your travels create interesting vignettes. But even if you haven't been on your dream vacation, you can still find pieces inspired by these places. Vintage globes automatically bring travel to mind. Maps make appealing artwork and are available in any size, from postcard to mural.

LEFT Wall hangings collected during travels are the focal point of this sitting room and an everyday reminder of a favorite vacation.

RIGHT An original portrait of a special family member adds whimsy to an otherwise sleek bedroom.

WALL WORDS This graphic element gives even nonartistic homeowners a way to add their favorite sayings and quotes to any wall. A one-time-use product, full words or single letters are available in a range of colors and fonts.

NATURAL ACCENTS A beautiful arrangement can be made of pressed leaves, shells you collected on a trip to the shore, interesting pods and seeds. Mount them in a shadow box, or put them under glass on a table. Don't overlook flowers and plants. Greenery is welcome in any space, and fresh flowers are always an inviting touch.

TOP LEFT A simple orchid is the perfect complement to the other pieces on this console table, softening the space and adding an organic touch.

TOP RIGHT A soulful twist on the conventional bulletin board, this antique-look metal display rack shows off a mix of personal mementos and vintage finds.

BOTTOM LEFT Tame chaotic piles of books by using unruly stacks to showcase objects of similar shapes and colors. Even the most haphazard piles will seem intentional.

BOTTOM RIGHT Group objects to tell a story. Retro wanderlust is the theme here, with a jet-plane-patterned soft pillow, vintage globe, and antique camera.

The Art of Display

On a shelf above Francesca Harris's desk, several small vintage clocks create a vignette next to silver picture frames and a collection of candles.

OPPOSITE PAGE, CLOCKWISE FROM TOP LEFT Ticking-stripe pillows bring depth to a white couch. Lucite and crystal candleholders and simple white candles bring sparkle to the bedside table. Identical frames add a sense of order, while the transparent lamp sets off the pristine white bookshelf and files. Vintage silver frames and antique mirrors share a similar patina atop a dresser. White china and earth-toned pottery fill the kitchen shelves; family art-work and photos are unexpected accents.

In Francesca Harris's home, family photos, treasured keepsakes, and everyday objects are celebrated in a simple yet striking way. Harris, a design-build contractor and home inspector in Corte Madera, California, believes in meaningful decor. "I'm obsessed with my family photos," she says. "I love making art out of memories."

Her secret is sticking to a black-and-white palette throughout the home. The walls are painted white, except for a glossy chocolate-brown accent wall in her bedroom. Furnishings are equally informal and crisp, and accessories were chosen to play off these neutrals.

To keep her aesthetic polished and classic, Harris buys three or four of the same frames at a time, always in black or white. The use of mass-market frames and mats gives her the freedom to swap photos in and out, and keeps her displays from feeling too precious.

Finally, Harris believes in collections rather than single objects. "Collections have more impact," she explains. These principles, and a disciplined hand, have resulted in a home that's rich with style and meaning.

The Elements

- **White Walls:** These provide a backdrop for the other elements of the house, and are easy to live with for the long term.

- **Doses of Color:** Color is used as a small, surprising accent, such as in rows of books grouped by color and displays of her sons' art projects.

- **Well-Chosen Accessories:** Harris looks for pieces in complementary materials, such as vintage chrome sconces behind the living room couch and the transparent acrylic resin lamp in the bedroom.

- **Collections:** These include crisp white magazine files, family photos in silver frames, and a collection of clocks, each grouped for greater impact.

Storage

When you have a place for everything, your home can be a calm refuge. Storage solutions can be as simple as shelves, wall hooks, and boxes, or as elaborate as custom-built wall units. No matter what type of storage you're looking for, choose well-designed pieces that are functional and match your personal decorating style.

Hidden storage starts with closets and pantries, but there are other options. Freestanding storage includes armoires and sideboards. These can be used for their original purposes of holding clothes or dishes, silverware, and linens; or be retrofitted to suit any need, from an entertainment center to a home office. A trunk can serve as a coffee table, and a wicker basket with a cover can be used as a nightstand. Fabric-covered file cabinets do double duty as end tables, and a rolling cart in the kitchen can hold linens, dishes, small appliances, even wine and wineglasses.

Built-in storage tailored to your needs is a great solution. Furniture designer Michael Hennessey suggests, "When planning for window seats, specify a flip top or cabinet front for extra storage."

Don't overlook display storage. Books open to view are a given, but you can display your grandmother's china, a teacup collection, photos or artwork, and other treasures in a glass-front cabinet or on shelves.

LEFT Bench seats and glass-front cabinets blend into this living space, thanks to the detailing that matches the window trim.

ABOVE, TOP Restaurant racks and plate holders become both functional and aesthetically pleasing elements in a kitchen when kept organized.

ABOVE, BOTTOM LEFT Smart storage beneath the sitting area keeps extra items, such as throws, pillows, and games, out of sight but easily accessible.

ABOVE, BOTTOM RIGHT A Murphy bed with built-in storage is the perfect solution for a small room that needs to house guests as well as other activities.

Chapter 7

Getting It Done

The previous chapters give a good grounding in the considerations that come into play when decorating your home. Now it's time to shift from dreaming mode into doing mode. You may choose to do it yourself or to work with a professional. Either way, the following pages will give you an idea of how to plan and budget for your project and offer you tips for working with professionals. Keep in mind that designing your home is a long-term process. Trends come and go—allow your home to evolve over time.

Gathering ideas, researching your options, and pulling together photos are all great ways to determine what you like and don't like. As you go through what you collected, you'll begin to see patterns: which colors appeal, the types of furniture you are drawn to, the overall style you prefer. This will help you create your final design.

Keeping binders and notebooks of the information you collect is a great tool throughout any decorating project. You will be able to refer to photos and notes throughout the process. You'll also be able to use these to explain your ideas and preferences to anyone you work with, whether it's a professional designer or a showroom salesperson. Having something to look at can prevent miscommunication and save hours of time.

Creating a Plan

The best results begin with an overall plan. Even if you're simply refurbishing the bathroom, you'll want to determine the order of work; for example, install a new vanity and faucet, paint the walls, put up new towel racks, then add finishing hardware.

If your project is larger, then having a plan is even more important. You don't want the new furniture sitting in the middle of the room while the walls are being painted. And if your project requires extensive remodeling, then you'll need to schedule work crews and be sure you get all required permits.

INTERIOR DESIGNER
KERRIE L. KELLY ON

Sharing Ideas

Don't be afraid to share your ideas with salespeople at the furniture stores, lighting experts, painters, and designers. The more information you can share, the more you will learn from the experts, and the better the chances that your project will turn out just as you'd hoped it would."

ABOVE Redoing a room doesn't mean starting from scratch. Sometimes little touches—changing the wall color, re-covering an armchair, or repainting a dresser—can have a huge impact.

RIGHT When planning a space that incorporates several rooms, take the time to choose colors, fixtures, and accessories that coordinate throughout. This often means planning ahead to allow for delivery time.

Creating a Schedule

It's obvious that you'll want a precise schedule for a large project. Any structural, electrical, or plumbing changes will need to be done before completing the wall finishes or adding light fixtures. Built-in pieces will need to be put into place before the flooring is installed. All these different parts of the puzzle need to be handled before you bring in the furniture and accessories.

For a large makeover, numerous people may come and go throughout the process. You'll want to be sure they are scheduled to arrive at a point where they can immediately get to work. You'll also want to ensure that the work one person is doing doesn't impede the progress of someone else.

On a small project, the schedule can be more informal. Even so, plan the steps you'll be taking, and figure out how long each should take. If you're new to this, especially if you are doing the work yourself, build in extra time.

If you order materials, furnishings, or accessories or have things made to order, find out when you should expect delivery. Delivery can often take several weeks, even for pieces that are not custom-made, so be sure you allow plenty of time.

Working with a Budget

No matter how large or how small your project is, you will want to know what the final cost will be. The budget depends on a number of factors, including how

extensive the changes will be, which types of materials and furnishings you choose, and whether you will do any portion of the work yourself, such as shopping for furniture and accessories or painting the room.

Realistically, you may have to prioritize your expenditures. To make the most of your budget, look for pieces you

love or finishes that make a statement, and spend most of your money there. You may be able to scale back on other, less noticeable pieces, or there may be alternatives that you like just as much but that aren't as expensive.

Look for other ways to make your dollars go further. This might include reusing some pieces, either in different ways or by repainting, restaining, or re-covering them. You may also need to wait to add one or two pieces. Look at this as an opportunity. Living with a room for a while will give you a better idea of what you truly need. And you never know what you might see later that will be perfect for the space.

Making It Work

The real fun is seeing how your design evolves. Take photos from beginning to end. It will be rewarding to look back to see how your idea came to life. Finally, don't rush and make choices without thinking them through. Instead, enjoy the entire design process by making it a journey, taking one step at a time.

Working with Professionals

There's no reason you can't handle a design project yourself if the changes are simple enough or your skills are strong. But you may want to hire professionals for the more complex parts of all of the jobs.

Hiring a Professional

People turn to design professionals for a variety of reasons. Most important is their knowledge of sources. Professionals have canvased the market and are able to obtain specialty goods on behalf of their clients. They can produce sample materials and finishes, photos and sketches, and renderings and schemes of the proposed finished space, allowing the client to visualize and approve concepts prior to starting the job. Working with professionals from the outset can spare you the frustration of managing multiple tradespeople for a project.

Professionals can assist with controlling the budget and making a time schedule for the project as well. Since redesigning or furnishing an area can be a significant expense, professionals can help you avoid costly aesthetic mistakes, ensuring the end product is both visually pleasing and functional.

Architects and designers can help you see a room in a different way. Shelving built into the wall turns unused space into a display niche.

although some have design skills as well. Other professionals you might want to hire to complete part of a project include painters, electricians, and plumbers.

Even if you need design help but can't afford a trained designer or architect—and don't assume that you can't without interviewing a few—don't overlook the design staffs at the places you shop. Although they may not be professionally trained, they know their products and can offer options you might not consider. Remember, though, their job is to sell their products, so evaluate their advice carefully.

When looking for a professional, it is wise to interview multiple candidates and ask for references, especially for a large project. Ask to see the work executed by the firm. Also be sure you feel you can work well with the person. More often than not, through the design process and after becoming acquainted with the preferences and needs of a client, the professional becomes a personal friend as well. Interior designer Jennifer Hilgardner says, "Houses become homes when all of the design ideas and aspects come together."

Contracts

Once you have found a person or firm you want to work with, you should have a contract that clearly states the job requirements, fee, and schedule. Smaller jobs that last only a few days might not require such a formal contract, although you should get fees and the schedule in writing.

Design professionals often charge about 10 percent of the total cost of the project (including materials) if they design the space, hire contractors, and oversee the installation. You can also choose to pay an hourly fee just for design.

The type of professional you might want depends on the scope of the project. Interior designers are experts in the nuances of different design styles and knowledgeable about the quality of furniture and other pieces. They can offer invaluable advice about overall layouts. There are also licensed designers who specialize in specific areas, such as bathrooms or kitchens.

If you're remodeling, you may want to enlist the help of an architect or a general contractor. Architects are state-licensed professionals who can create structurally sound and workable designs. General contractors specialize in construction,

ARCHITECT
CLAY AURELL ON

Working with Clients

As an architect, my favorite part of the business is the professional-client relationship and seeing clients walk through their projects. It can be very rewarding for both parties. Clients pour their heart and soul into their new project, and a thoughtful professional will work with the clients to help them realize their dreams and exceed their expectations. The architect or designer has the opportunity to take a multitude of ideas, magazine clippings, fabrics, artwork, and items that are dear to the client, analyze them, and create an amazing space out of everything."

Resources

The following are organizations, associations, manufacturers, and retailers mentioned in this book along with a variety of others you might find helpful when designing your home decor. The emphasis is on companies dedicated to environmentally responsible manufacturing processes and/or products.

Organizations and Associations

American Society of Interior Designers
asid.org
The oldest and largest organization of interior design professionals. The Web site includes advice on hiring a designer and green design.

California Building Industry Association
cbia.org
The California Building Industry Association is a statewide trade association representing more than 5,000 companies, including home builders, trade contractors, architects, engineers, designers, suppliers, and other industry professionals.

ENERGY STAR
energystar.gov
The Web site of the joint program of the Environmental Protection Agency and the Department of Energy offers information and guidance on product selection and home improvements for energy savings.

Forest Stewardship Council
fsc.org
An independent, nonprofit organization established to promote the responsible management of the world's forests.

Sustainable Furnishings Council
sustainablefurnishings.org
A nonprofit coalition that promotes sustainable practices among manufacturers, retailers, and consumers.

WaterSense
epa.gov/watersense
A program that identifies high-efficiency fixtures.

Manufacturers and Retailers

Accent on Closets
accentonclosets.com
Manufacturer of storage systems for bathrooms, bedrooms, home offices, garages, kitchens, and family and living rooms.

All American Design & Furnishings, Inc.
allamericandesignand furnishings.com
Design firm offering interior and exterior planning and installation services.

Arizona Tile
arizonatile.com
Importer of over 230 varieties of granite, marble, limestone, travertine, slate, and onyx slabs and tile.

Armstrong
armstrong.com
Best known for its flooring products, which include hardwoods, laminates, ceramic tile, vinyl, and linoleum. Armstrong also offers a range of ceiling products and a line of stock cabinets.

Benjamin Moore
benjaminmoore.com
Quality paint manufacturer that now offers a line of low-odor, low-VOC paints.

Berkeley Mills
berkeleymills.com
An FSC-certified furnituremaker.

Carlisle Wide Plank Floors
wideplankflooring.com
Makers of historical-style wood flooring in a variety of hardwoods and reclaimed woods.

Catalina Home

catalinahome.com
Manufacturer of carpets, rugs, wood flooring, and tile, including eco-friendly options.

C.G. Sparks

cgsparks.com
C.G. Sparks, Furniture with Soul, designs and manufactures furnishings that are beautiful, useful, and long-lived. The company's line also includes accessories, rugs, and Indian and Tibetan antiques.

Coalesse

coalesse.com
Designer of furniture that bridges the gap between the living room and the home office.

Danze

danze.com
Plumbing supplier offering a large range of kitchen and bathroom fixtures, mirrors, vanities, and accessories in a range of styles and finishes.

EcoTimber

ecotimber.com
A supplier of sustainably harvested wood, reclaimed wood, and bamboo floors.

Environmental Products and Design

environmental products-design.com
A good source for nontoxic and environmentally responsible building and design products, from tile and paint to furniture and tableware.

Expanko

expanko.com
Resource for a range of cork products, recycled rubber, and flooring made from a combination of cork and rubber.

Forbo

forbo-flooring.com
Source for Marmoleum™ linoleum flooring.

Heath Ceramics

heathceramics.com
Legendary midcentury pottery company that manufactures tiles and tableware under stringent self-imposed recycling and reuse programs.

Kohler

kohler.com
A recognized leader in kitchen and bath design.

Kyle Bunting Rugs

kylebunting.com
Designer and manufacturer of cowhide rugs, upholstery, wall coverings, and furniture panels.

Lumens Light + Living

lumens.com
Supplier of European- and American-designed lighting, fans, and home accessories; the company also showcases studio glassmakers, artisan lampmakers, and small design studios.

MANDALA Tile

mandalatile.com
Supplier of luxury tile from around the world.

Natural Stone Design Gallery

nsdgallery.com
Supplier of ceramic, porcelain, and glass tile as well as metal and stone accents, shellstone, travertine, quartzite, slate, granite, marble, and limestone materials.

Oceanside Glasstile

glasstile.com
Manufacturer and supplier of handcrafted artisan glass tiles and trim.

The Old Fashioned Milk Paint Co.

milkpaint.com
Maker of chemically safe, historically authentic paint.

Reclaim

reclaimhome.com
Retail supplier of healthy, eco-friendly products for the entire home.

Rejuvenation

rejuvenation.com
Manufacturer of period reproduction light fixtures, hardware, and house parts; the company also deals in architectural salvage.

Roppe

roppe.com
Source for rubber floor tiles and more.

Sunbrella

sunbrella.com
The leading manufacturer of outdoor fabrics.

Swaim

swaim-inc.com
Manufacturer of contemporary furniture based on classic designs.

TerraMai

terramai.com
Producer of flooring and other products from wood reclaimed from a variety of sources, including old buildings and bridges, railroad ties, and abandoned logging operations.

Toto

totousa.com
Manufacturer of tubs, toilets, sinks, faucets, and showerheads.

Trestlewood

trestlewood.com
Dealer in reclaimed wood planks and beams.

Walker Zanger

walkerzanger.com
Manufacturer and supplier of stone and ceramic tile and architectural glass collections.

Wall Words

wallwords.com
Supplier of prepasted, prespaced letters and graphics for painted walls, wallpaper, windows, mirrors, furniture, and metal.

The Woods Company

thewoodscompany.com
Manufacturer of flooring from antique wood.

YOLO Colorhouse

yolocolorhouse.com
Creator of high-quality, zero-VOC paint with a natural palette.

Credits

Photography

American Clay Enterprises: 125BL and BR; Edmund Barr: 175B; Laurie Black: 97BR; Rob D. Brodman: 39T, 111TR; courtesy of Kyle Bunting (kylebunting.com): 45TL, 152 both; Harry Chamberlain: 15TR, 23TR; ©2009 Ciro Coelho/cirocoelho.com: 49BR, 59TR, 65T, 88, 89 both, 118T, 180; courtesy of Coalesse (coalesse.com): 100BR, 101T; Beverly Bozarth Colgan: 137; Susan Corry: 55B, 184BR; Fred Donham, Photographer Link (photographerlink.com): 3M, 18R, 19T, 50, 52 both, 61B, 77BR, 80TL, 105TR, 135BL, 143, 150, 157BL, 163TR, 164T, 165TL, 168BL, 171B, 173, 179; Emeraldlight/Corbis: 97TL; Hal Finkelstein: 155TR; Vance Fox©Vance Fox Photography, courtesy of Del Webb Sierra Canyon: 99T, 185TR; courtesy of Furnitalia: 163BR, 164B, 165B, 166BL and BR; Tria Giovan: 175M; Thayer Allyson Gowdy: 81 all; Jay Grahan: 97MR; John Granen: 39B, 99BR, 144, 192, 207; Art Gray: 109TR; Alex Hayden: 103T, 103M, 146BL; Robin G. Heard: 119BR; Steven Holmes Creative: 4R, 5TL, 5TML, 5TR, 5BML, 133T, 176, 177 all, 182; Rob Karosis: 3L, 22, 28TL, 28TR, 29, 31TL, 33, 63BR, 65B, 66, 84R, 87TL, 102, 117B, 122BL, 123, 129T, 129BL, 131B, 133B, 139, 162, 168T, 197, 198, 199; Kerrie L. Kelly: 23TL, 25M; Muffy Kibbey: 68B, 97TR; courtesy of KlipTech Composites: 72B; Michiko

Kurisu: 154, 155B; Warren Lieb: 63MR, 101B, 110BL; Jennifer Mau: 49BL, 64; Emily Nathan: 189BR; Alise O'Brien Photography: 46T; Salvador Ochoa (salvadorochoa.com): 59MR, 69T, 77TR, 83T, 109TL; Lea O'Shea, SLR Photography (slr-photo.com): 34; Dr. John Roberts: 13; Lisa Romerein: 131TL, 134, 169; Eric Roth: 2L, 2R, 3R, 7, 8, 9 both, 10, 11B, 12 both, 14, 15BR, 16 all, 17, 18L, 19B, 20T, 20M, 21T, 23B, 24, 25B, 26 both, 28B, 30 both, 31TR, 31B, 32, 38, 41, 42, 43BL, 44, 47 both, 49TR, 56B, 57, 59BR, 60, 61TL, 61TR, 62, 67T, 74, 75 both, 76, 78, 79 all, 80B, 82, 83BL, 85L, 92, 93T, 96B, 105BR, 107, 115, 116, 119T, 120, 121M, 121B, 122TM, 124, 125TL, 126T, 127 all, 128, 130TR, 132, 140, 141MR, 145 all, 146T, 147, 151B, 156, 167L, 181, 184BL, 187B, 188, 189T, 189ML, 193 all, 195, 196; Cesar Rubio: 161; Stuart Ruckman Photography: 40R, 51R, 165TR; Ron Ruscio Photography: 87B; Claudio Santini: 43BR; Pablo Sipala: 141TR; Michael Skott: 21B, 35, 129BR, 168BR, 183, 185BR, 200; Thomas J. Story: 1, 37, 39M, 40L, 43TL, 43TR, 45R, 46B, 48 both, 49TL, 54, 55T, 56T, 58, 68TL , 68TR, 69B, 70BL, 71TR, 72T, 73 all, 80TR, 83BR, 84L, 87TR, 90 both, 91 both, 93B, 94L, 96TL, 96TR, 98, 99BL, 100T, 100BL, 103B, 104, 106 both, 108, 109BR, 110TL, 110TR, 110BR, 112, 113 all, 122TL, 122TR, 122BR, 125TR, 126B, 130L, 130MR, 135BR,

136B, 146BR, 148, 149L, 149R, 157TL, 157TM, 157TR, 158, 159R, 167R, 172, 174, 175T, 186, 187T, 189MR, 189BL, 190, 191 all; Tim Street-Porter: 20B, 25T, 27, 53, 119BL, 136T, 141BR, 153, 184T, 202, 204; Cathi Taraboi, Cathi Taraboi Photography: 65M; courtesy of Tileshop Inc. in Berkeley, CA, and Mirage Granito Ceramico in Italy: 151TR; E. Spencer Toy: 130BL, 130BR; Roger Turk, Northlight Photography: 63TR; Dominique Vorillon: 70TR; courtesy of Walker & Zanger, Inc.: 117T, 117M, 151TL, 185L; Rip Williams: 121T; Michele Lee Willson (styling by Laura Del Fava): 85M, 86TR, 86BR, 95, 135TR; courtesy of Yolo Colorhouse: 45BL

Design

1: Cisco Pinedo, Cisco Brothers; 2L: Morse Constructions, Inc.; 3R: Christine Lane Interiors; 3M: Kerrie L. Kelly, All American Design & Furnishings, Inc.; 7: Morse Constructions, Inc.; 8: Mark Christofi Interiors; 9T: Design Elements Interior Design; 9B: Seimasko + Verbridge; 10: Mark Christofi Interiors; 11T: Rana Maheri-Desar, LEED AP, Allied ASID; 11B: Pappas Miron; 12 both: AbbyK, Inc.; 13: Kristen Phillips, Bellissimo Décor; 14: Eck MacNeely Architects, Inc.; 15TR: Marlene Oliphant Design; 15BR: Mark Christofi Interiors; 16T: JW Construction, Inc.; 16BL: Mark Christofi Interiors; 17: Pappas Miron; 18R & 19T: Kerrie L. Kelly, All American Design & Furnishings, Inc.; 21T: Carter & Co. Interior Design; 22: Pi Smith and John Vansant, Smith & Vansant Architects; 23TL: Kerrie L. Kelly, All American Design & Furnishings, Inc.; 23TR: Marlene Oliphant Design; 23B: Benjamin Nutter Architects, LLC; 25T: Zoltan Pali, SPF Architects; 25M: Kerrie L. Kelly, All American Design & Furnishings, Inc.; 25B: Sebastian Carpenter Design; 27: Greg Mimmaugh; 28TL: Pi Smith and John Vansant, Smith & Vansant Architects; 28TR: DPF Design, Inc. (Ann Sargent, Martha von Ammon, Denise Welch); 28B: Chris Walsh and Co., Architects, Inc.; 29: Pi Smith and John Vansant, Smith & Vansant Architects; 30T and B: Blutz + Klug; 31TL: James Crisp, Crisp Architects; 31TR:

Susan Sargent; 31B: Britta Design Inc.; 33: Pi Smith and John Vansant, Smith & Vansant Architects; 34: Sara Robertson Design; 37: Kelly Barthelemy Design; 38: Christine Lane Interiors; 39T: Lindy Small Architecture; 39M: Lara Dutto, D-Cubed; 39B: Kevin Price, J.A.S. Design-Build; 40L: Catherine Bailey and Robin Petravic; 40R: Interior Architecture & Design by Ron Godwin & Associates. Furniture by C. G. Sparks; 43TL and TR: Architect: Faulkner Architects. Interior Design: Spirit Interior Design (Cathy Nason, ASID, and Katherine Elkins); 43BR: David Coleman, Architecture; 45TL: Design and rug design: Neri & Hu; 45R: Design: Dirk Stennick; Lighting and furniture: Jacqueline Bucelli Designs; Colors and finishes: Patty Glikbarg, Pannagan Designs; 45BL: Yolo Colorhouse; 46T: Christy Knapp and Michelle Triplett, Edwin Pepper Interiors; 46B: Lindy Small Architecture; 47B: Seimasko + Verbridge; 48T: McDonald & Moore. Furniture: Room and Board; 48B: Daniel Germani, BD&M; 49BL: Norma S. Zeigler, ASID, Entwine Interiors; 49BR: Clay Aurell, AB Design Studio; 50: Kerrie L. Kelly, All American Design & Furnishings, Inc.; 51R: Interior Architecture and Design by Ron Godwin and Associates. Furniture by C. G. Sparks; 52T and B: Kerrie L. Kelly, All American Design & Furnishings, Inc.; 53: Maxine Greenspan; 54: Cary Bernstein Architect; 55T: McDonald & Moore; 55B: Susan Corry Design; 56T: Pamela Pennington Studios; 57: Heather G. Wells, Ltd.; 58: McDonald & Moore; 59TR: Clay Aurell, AB Design Studio; 59MR: Kerrie L. Kelly, All American Design & Furnishings, Inc.; 59BR: Good Interiors; 60: Thayne Emrich Design LLC; 61B: Kerrie L. Kelly, All American Design & Furnishings, Inc.; 62: Mark Christofi Interiors; 63TR: Natalia Smith Idée Chic Design; 63MR: Dominick Tringali Architects Inc.; 63BR: Architect/Builder: Warner McCounaughey, HammerSmith Design; 64: Norma S. Zeigler, ASID, Entwine Interiors; 65T: Clay Aurell, AB Design Studio; 65M: Carla Aston Aston Design Studio; 65B: Rob Whitten, Whitten Architects;

66: Architect: Little Green Homes; Designer/Craftsman: Chris Dennen, Dennen Design; 67T: Seimasko + Verbridge; 68TL: DeWitt Residential Design and Interiors; 68TR: Pamela Pennington Studios; 68B: Christine Curry Designs; 69T: Kerrie L. Kelly, All American Design & Furnishings, Inc.; 69B: Dirk Stennick Designs; 70TR: Kathryn Ireland; 72T: Design: Liz Olberding; Design/Construction: Tom Kelly, Neil Kelly Co.; Interior Design: Therese DuBravac, Neil Kelly Co.; 72B: PaperStone; 73TL: Michelle Kaufman Designs; 73TR: Pamela Pennington Studios; 73B: Sierra Design/Architecture; 74–75: Heather G. Wells, Ltd.; 76: Benjamin Nutter Architects, LLC; 77TR and BR: Kerrie L. Kelly, All American Design & Furnishings, Inc.; 78: Good Interiors; 79TL: JW Construction, Inc.; 79R: Chris Walsh and Co., Architects, Inc.; 80TL: Kerrie L. Kelly, All American Design & Furnishings, Inc.; 80TR: Pamela Pennington Studios; 83T: Kerrie L. Kelly, All American Design & Furnishings, Inc.; 83BL: Benjamin Nutter Architects, LLC; 83BR: Dick Stennick Design; 84L: DeWitt Residential Design and Interiors; 84R: Architect: Barbara Winslow, JSW/D Architects; 85R: Cabinets by Michael Meyer Fine Woodworking, Bay West Builders, William Duff Architects; 86TR: Design by Regina Interiors; Behrens Curry, Inc., builders; 86BR: Anne Laird-Blanton, architect; 87TL: DPF Design, Inc. (Ann Sargent, Martha Von Ammon, Denise Welch); 87TR: Cisco Pinedo, Cisco Brothers; 87B: Jennifer A. Jelinek, JJ Interiors, LLC; 88–89: Clay Aurell, AB Design Studio; 90L: Architect: Siegal & Strain Architects, DeWitt; 90R: Anna Labbee. J.A.S. Design-Build; 91L: Jensen & Macy Architects; 91R: Michelle Kaufman Designs; 92: Eck MacNeely Architects, Inc.; 93B: Pamela Pennington Studios; 94L: Lara Dutto, D-Cubed; 95: Kathryn Rogers, Sogno Design Group; Lawrence Construction Co.; Anglisse Karol; 96TL: A & D Architecture + Design; 96TR: Kenneth Brown Design; 97TL: Lorcan O'Herlihy, architect; 97MR: Jeffry L. Day/Min-Day and Marc Toma and Lisa K. Trujillo (BerksToma

Architects); Interior Design by Marie Fisher and Alissa Ullie (Marie Fisher Interior Design); 97TR: Arnold Mammarella, architect; Marcy Voyevod, Interior Design; construction by Elon Ersch; lighting by Marcee Shefren; 97BR: Jill Lewis and Lane Williams, Coop 15; 98: Paris Renfroe Design; 99T: Kerrie L. Kelly, All American Design & Furnishings, Inc.; 99BL: Architect/Interior Designer: John Lum Architecture; Builder: Meridian Builders & Developers; 99BR: Kevin Price, J.A.S. Design-Build; 100T: Eszter Rabin; 100BL: Joe and Kalli Rivers Altieri; 101B: Dominick Tringali Architects Inc.; 102: Smith & Vansant Architects; 103T and M: Jenny Beedon Snow and Brett Snow; 103B: Tamm Jasper Interiors; 104: Nahemow Rivera Group; 105TR: Kerrie L. Kelly, All American Design & Furnishings, Inc.; 106T: Annie Speck, Interior Design; 106B: Nahemow Rivera Group; 107: Benjamin Nutter Architects, LLC; 108: Eric Trabert & Associates. Architects; Builder: Mulvaney & Co.; Interior Design: Annie Speck Interior Designs; Accessories: Tuvalu Home Environment; 109TL: Kerrie L. Kelly, All American Design & Furnishings Inc.; 109TR: PaysonDenny Architects; 109BR: Builder: Mark DeMattei and DeMattei Constructions; Architect: Dahlin Group Architecture and Planning; Interior Design: McDonald & Moore; Landscape Architect: Nuvis Landscape Architecture and Planning; 110TL: Siegel & Strain Architects, Dewitt; 110TR: Julie Higgs and Dave Stricker; 110BL: Dominick Tringali Architects Inc.; 110BR: Vermeil Design; 111TR: Landscape Design: Vanessa Kuenmerle, Vee Horticulture; 112–113: Antonio Martins Interior Design; 117B: The Nantucket Beadboard Co.; 118T: Clay Aurell, AB Design Studio; 119T: Thayne Emrich Design LLC; 119BL: Thomas Calloway and Associates; 119BR: Robin Heard Design; Ernie R. Sanchez; 121T: Elizabeth Hunter, Design Diva; 121B: Duffy Design Group; 122TL: Douglas Thornley, Gould Evans Baum Thornley Architects; 122TM: Pappas Miron; 122TR: Byron Kuth and Elizabeth

Ramieri, Kuth/Ramieri Architects; Construction: Tommy Hicks and Chris Whitney; 122BR: Ann Bertelsen; Styling by Emma Star Jensen; 122BL: DPF Design, Inc. (Ann Sargent, Martha Von Ammon, Denise Welch); 125TR: D. Patrick Finnigan; Shower plaster: BMI Products of Northern California; 126T: Linda Taylor Interiors; 126B: Yolo Colorhouse; 127L: Seimasko + Verbridge; 128: Cindy Seeley Designs; 129T: TMS Architects, William Soupcoff; 129BL: Smith & Vansant Architects; 130MR: Architect: Faulkner Architects, Builder: Robert Marr Construction; Interior Design: Spirit Interior Design (Cath Nason, ASID and Katherine Elkins); 131TL: Molly Luetkemeyer, M. Design Interiors; 131B: Rob Whitten, Whiten Architects; 132: Seimasko + Verbridge; 133T: Kerrie L. Kelly, All American Design & Furnishings, Inc.; 133B: Architect/Builder: Warner McCounaughey, Hammer-Smith Design; 134: Vanessa De Varga; 135TR: Brian Eby; 135BL: Kerrie L. Kelly, All American Design & Furnishings, Inc.; 135BR: Francesca Quagliata, 4th Street Design; 136T: Tim Clarke; 136B: Jess Chamberlain; 139: Smith & Vansant Architects; 140: Kelly McGuill Home; 141TR: Jeanine Naviaux, On the Inside Design; 141BR: Warren Wagner, W3 Architects; 142: Christine E. Barnes; 143: Kerrie L. Kelly, All American Design & Furnishings, Inc.; 144: John Schneider and Kim Clements, J.A.S. Design-Build; 145TL: Christine Lane Interiors: 145TR: Seimasko + Verbridge; 145B: Chris Walsh and Co., Architects, Inc.; 146T: Susan Sargent; 146BL HhLodesign; 146BR: Francesca Quagliata, 4th Street Design; 147: Benjamin Nutter Architects, LLC; 148–149: Yolo Colorhouse; 150: Kerrie L. Kelly, All American Design & Furnishings, Inc.; 152T: Design: Re:think Design Studio; rug design: Neri & Hu; 152B: Design: Campion Platt; rug design: Neri & Hu; 154–155: Susan Cozzi, Susan Cozzi Design Studio Inc.; 157TL and BL: Kerrie L. Kelly, All American Design & Furnishings, Inc.; 157TM: Design: Charles de Lisle, Your Space Interiors. Architect: Heidi Richardson, Richardson Architects; 157TR: Kelly

Barthelemy Design; 158–159: Design: Fergus Garber Group, Michel Biehn, La Maison Biehn, France; 161: Nick Noyes Architecture; 162: Rob Whitten, Whitten Architects; 163TR, 164T, and 165TL: Kerrie L. Kelly, All American Design & Furnishings, Inc.; 165TR and 166T: C. G. Sparks; 167R: Lara Dutto, D-Cubed; 168BL: Kerrie L. Kelly, All American Design & Furnishings Inc.; 169: Lewis/Schoeplein Architects; 170 and 171T: Furnitalia; 171B: Kerrie L. Kelly, All American Design & Furnishings, Inc.; 172: Safdie Rabines Architects; 173: Kerrie L. Kelly, All American Designs & Furnishings, Inc.; 175T: Design: Francesca Quagliata, 4th Street Design; 175M: Philip Sides Interior Design, Harrison Design Associates. Construction by Southeastern Construction and Management; 175B: Ellis A. Schoicher, EASA Architecture; Bess Wiersema and Megan Matthews, Studio 3 Design; 176–177, 179: Kerrie L. Kelly, All American Design & Furnishings, Inc.; 180: Clay Aurell, AB Design Studio; 184T: Roy McMakin; 184BL: Christine Lane Interiors; 184BR: Susan Corry Design; 185TR: Kerrie L. Kelly, All American Design & Furnishings, Inc.; 186: Francesca Quagliata, 4th Street Design; 187T: Pamela Hill and Lois MacKenzie, Otto Baat Group; 187B: AbbyK, Inc.; 188: JW Construction, Inc.; 189MR: Kelly Barthelemy Design; 189BL: Styling by Miranda Jones; 189BR: Velocity Art and Design; 190–191: Francesca Harris, FHIG; 192: Design: Kevin Price, J.A.S. Design-Build, Color work: Kim Clements, J.A.S. Design-Build; 193T: Kelly McGuill Home; 195: Christine Lane Interiors; 196: Two Ton, Inc.; 197: Design: Carolyn Tierney and Diane Susoev, Ferrium Design Studio; Architect: James Crisp, Crisp Architects; 198: Design: DPF Design, Inc. (Ann Sargent, Martha von Ammon, Denise Welch); 199: Pi Smith and John Vansant, Smith & Vansant Architects; 202T: Warren Wagner, W3 Architects; 204: Design: Liz Olberding, Design/Construction: Tom Kelly, Neil Kelly Co. Interior Design: Therese DuBravac; 207: Joe Schneider and Kim Clements, J.A.S. Design-Build

Index